OMNIVORES

Alfa-Scott Olson

Marshall Efron

OMNIVORES

THEY SAID THEY
WOULD EAT ANYTHING—
AND THEY *DID!*

by

Alfa-Betty Olsen

and

Marshall Efron

with

AN AFFIDAVIT

by

MEL BROOKS

and

VISUAL GARNI

by

RON BARRETT

THE VIKING PRESS / NEW YORK

Library of Congress Cataloging in Publication Data

Olsen, Alfa-Betty.
Omnivores.

1. Food. I. Efron, Marshall, joint author.
II. Title.
TX355.048   641'.013   78-23414
ISBN 0-670-46570-4

Printed in the United States of America
Set in Linotype Helvetica Light

Portions of this book originally appeared in *Esquire, Moneysworth,*
and *Soho Weekly News,* in somewhat different form.

We would like to dedicate this book to John Engels,
the poet (not to be confused with John Engels, the
sanitation man), for his valuable guidance, encour-
agement, and assistance.

Special thanks to Barbara Burn for her patience
and her trust in us.

Preface

THE ARGUMENT

Having examined the book-club offerings and the lists of the many publishing houses all over this great land of ours—to say nothing of looking in magazines—we have concluded that nothing has been written about food lately, that altogether too few people have really thought seriously about the subject and, taking the world as a whole, that many have not even heard of the stuff and are in danger of starvation through ignorance.

RESOLUTION

We have, therefore, dedicated a year of our lives (the best year) to the pursuit of savories and to the discovery of the principles and particles behind them.

COMPLAINT

Our course has been the lonely road, the highway on which few pass, the avenue that leads to exotic and strange out-of-the-way places: the corner grocery and the kitchen. Not one day has gone by when we did not consume food in one way or another. This book is the result of our travail.

EXHORTATION

So read on, reader, and let us pass along to you the accumulated thoughts, wisdom, knowledge and insight of our year in food.

GUARANTEE

We hereby affirm that every word of this book is either true or made up.

Contents

AN AFFIDAVIT

I, Mel Brooks
personally,
swear by almighty God that what I am about to say is the truth, the whole truth and almost nothing but the truth. Yes, I have seen them eat. Both of them. I have seen Miss Olsen, whom I have known since 1967 when we were both working on *The Producers,* eat more often than I have seen Mr. Efron eat. Seeing her eat is instructive, but seeing *him* eat is both instructive and terrifyng!

They eat with energy, youthful exultancy and utter recklessness—con gusto and con carne. And what application, style and violence! I have seen him chase a pea around a plate with a knife for fifteen minutes before tiring. They are both capable of stripping chicken bones to the white with just a knife and fork. The bones lie on the plate as cleanly denuded as if attacked by the Marabunta ants, who are known for their rapacious love of thighs and breasts.* And who else would have thought of eating Mexican food with chopsticks?

Watching them eat has given me an appreciation of table manners I never had before and has led me to the formulation of the Mel Brooks Six Rules of Dining Etiquette.

---

* Those living in a known Marabunta region should keep their thighs and breasts covered at all times.

1

Always keep your mouth closed while masticating.
(Masticating.)
Most people get disgusted when other people
discharge sardine fragments on them.
I say "most people" because there are always a few
who like it.

2

Once something is in your mouth,
you must swallow it. Yes.
Do not remove it to see what it is
or what it looks like.
Unless, of course, it is a bad clam.

3

When serving yourself at a buffet,
do not touch other people to make a point.

4

If you choke on a fish bone, leave the table quickly.
However, if you are choking on a chicken bone
you may stay.

5

When serving yourself at a buffet,
always return the serving spoons to the platter.
If, however, you should make a serious blunder
and walk away with the utensils, then bluff it through
by saying in a loud voice,
"It's just not dinner without a big spoon."

6

Do not shout,
"Gangway, all ashore that's going ashore,"
when the gravy boat comes in.

These are the six lucky rules that have guided my dining
career. If you want them you can commit them to memory, learn
them by rote, or write them on your cuff or the hem of your skirt

before you eat again. Then eat this page (if you are reading the limited gift edition, the pages are made of rice paper), and then go right out and buy another copy of this book because you'll want to know what's in the rest of it.

How should you read this book? Easy. Like you eat good, rich food. You should take a nibble, let it satisfy you. Later on, when you are hungry for something delicious, come back for another bite.

This is a book that will profoundly interest anyone who has ever been hungry.

Bon appetit,

Your humble servant,

Mel Brooks

New York
Paris
Lisbon
Beverly Hills

YOU DESERVE
A STEAK TODAY

If we were
going to spend a
year in food, we felt it would be an important gesture to try the most popular and the most common food experience in America today. So we hied ourselves off to our local McDonald's. The plan was to begin at the bottom and work our way sideways to the sublime—or the sub-slime, depending on how you feel about fattened goose liver, an adventure we planned for later on.

Our McDonald's has a sign outside that reads, "Shoes and shirts required," so the day we went there for lunch we were careful to wear both. We supposed that if you wore a tie, you'd be asked to leave.

On the way there we ran into Sidney, the world's oldest newsboy, selling some of the world's oldest newspapers. Sidney was one of the original Bohos in bohemian Greenwich Village and has managed to hang on and in ever since. Wearing an old tweed overcoat, as bearded as Rip Van Winkle ever was, his head bare except for his thick white hair, he peddles his wares from coffee shop to saloon and back again. Every evening, come rain or come shine, Sidney shambles from one establishment to another and from table to table with his bundle of outdated periodicals under his arm crying, "Last call for Art/Culture, last call for Art/Culture!"

1

When he saw us on the street, he made his pitch: "Hey, do you want last year's *Village Voice*? I got two from February and one from October. How about a copy of *Monocle*? The cover is missing but the rest is intact. Here's a new copy of *Antaeus,* I found it on the bus." We settled on two 1965 *Playboys* and an *Antioch Review* with Maxwell Bodenheim's autograph on the cover but nothing of his work on the inside. When we told Sidney we were going to McDonald's, he said, "I believe there was a McDonald's on Perry Street around nineteen-twenty-nine or thirty. A speakeasy. John O'Hara used to go there. Also Frank O'Hara and Scarlett O'Hara."

We said, "No, no. This one's a cafeteria. Nothing alcoholic there—except some of the customers."

Sidney's eyes dimmed. "Oh, the old days. There used to be a cafeteria on Sheridan Square. You could get a nickel cup

2

of coffee in a thick porcelain cup, sit around for hours, hear some good talk and watch the poets come and go." He pulled on his old grey beard reflectively. "Times have changed. The old days are going." As he left us, he called back, "I used to date Edna St. Vincent Millay!"

Well, he's right. Times *have* changed. The first person we saw in McDonald's was a crazy-lady, a true berserker, an angry woman. She was there for her twenty-cent cup of coffee, sitting at a window table—a great location strategically because she was in a position to abuse the people inside with her invective and simultaneously make ugly faces at the people passing out-side—doing her very own special thing.

We noted that the twenty-cent cup of coffee she was drinking generated quite a large pile of trash on her table. No more the large porcelain cup that you give back. Oh, no. This is a dis-posable cup (with a plastic pry-up lid, also disposable) that you can keep. Then there are the two half-and-half containers with rip-off tops, the three paper packets of granulated sugar, the two paper napkins and the plastic spoon for stirring your coffee. All disposable, all resting atop the disposable sheet of paper that serves as a placemat on the tray.

And every single item previously enumerated has the special twin arches and McDonald's logo on it (so you never forget where you're eating), thus creating monogrammed trash. Mc-Donald's advertises, "You deserve a break today." We like to think about the backs of the garbage collectors when we hear that.

And now for our lunch. We waited on line for it. And while waiting we counted thirty blue-uniformed workers on the other side of the counter, and still the service was slow. Be-sides that, the other four lines, identical to ours, moved faster than ours. It was like at the bank or the post office.

When we finally were waited upon, we decided to forego the filet-o-fish (don't ask what kind of fish, this is the generic not the specific, but at any rate, no matter how they blend it, it is pronounced filetto fish), and we both ordered Big Macs, choco-late shakes and french fries—the classic combo.

Having secured our lunch, we next found a table, sat down and started our own pile of litter. In order to get to the Big

3

Mac we first had to rip open the red box that bore the legend "recyclable paper" on the flap. What it did not tell us was whether it had been recycled or whether it was going to be recycled. Merely that it was capable of being recycled. We suspect that this is true of all paper.

Once we'd reached our food, we tinkered with it. We removed the middle layer of bread in the Big Mac, thus bringing the two little pieces of meat closer together, vastly improving the ratio of bread to meat and reducing the calorie count.

The Big Mac is inherently or intrinsically a double-decker sandwich. Crudely described:

$$P(A+B+A+B+A)P = BM$$

Precisely defined:

$$P(A+F+C+B+A+D+F+B+E+F+A)P = BM$$

P = paper, A = bread, B = meat patty, C = chopped lettuce, D = onions, E = sauce, F = pickle, BM = Big Mac

Or, to put it another way, the ratio of bread to meat is three to two in favor of bread. We liked equalizing that relationship and making it two to two.

Now for the big question. How did we like the Big Mac? Well, the bun is bland, not what you would call a terrific bread experience. The sauce has been described by international taste expert Dorian Treadway as "somehow like Thousand Island dressing" or "mayonnaise *rémoulade*" or "Olde English Furniture Polishe." We think it is closer to Russian dressing, although when a drop landed on our neighbor's shoe and he rubbed it with his thumb, he ended up with a hell of a shine.

But when you come to the meat, you come to the elusive heart of the hamburger question. And here at McDonald's we discovered a diminutive meat patty truly without any flavor. Texture, yes. Presence, yes—what there was of it. But flavor, no. Not really. Only people who have never had meat in any other form would call this meat meat. We don't know exactly what they do to it, but it is what we would call "distressed meat." Fortunately there isn't much, so it doesn't make much difference.

We watched as one customer came back to the counter with

4

his quarter-pounder. He said that the meat wasn't a quarter of a pound, it was less. The uniformed counter people told him to read the box. The meat was a quarter of a pound before it was cooked. After it is cooked is another story. The poor fellow walked away a little wiser, a little sadder, a little older.

So we suggest that people who buy the quarter-pounder should also buy the thirty-three-cent original McDonald's Hamburger. The thirty-three-cent original offering of the McDonald's chain is a large bun and a small piece of meat—maybe a sixteenth of a quarter-pounder before it is cooked. After it is cooked, maybe it's a thirty-second of a quarter-pounder. By combining both these hamburgers people will be certain to get their money's worth in bread.

Used to be, by the way, that the hamburger patty in the original cheap thirty-three-cent McDonald's was so small, a vegetarian could eat there without compromising his or her principles.

All in all, the Big Macs we ate tasted like Big Macs everywhere. That's one thing about McDonald's—you've tasted one, you've tasted them all. Or, to coin a joke, "Twenty minutes after you've finished dining at McDonald's, you want Chinese food."

Out on the street in search of further entertainment we amused ourselves by playing the Life Game. The Life Game went like this:

Miss Olsen started things off by saying, "Life is like a dead sea apple—it turns to ashes in your mouth."

Mr. Efron replied, "Life is like a two-by-four to the back of your head."

Miss Olsen said, "Life is like a McDonald's, the sum of its trash is equal to the whole of its trash."

Mr. Efron said, "Life is like a meal at McDonald's, a waste of time."

Miss Olsen said, "No, no. Nothing is a waste of time, especially life. Always remember: Never to have died is better than to have never lived at all."

We could have gone on like that forever because life in its infinite variety and exquisite agony offers a cornucopia of inspiration, but we didn't. We went to a Chinese restaurant instead.

THE GARLIC
REPORT

**e are really
quite fond of**
garlic, not only because it tastes so good, but because it illus-
trates a metaphysical truth: For every pleasure in life, there is
an opposite and equal displeasure. It's like Newton's Third Law:
Every action has an action opposite to itself of equal force.
With garlic the penalty is bat's breath. (Too much Tabasco, on
the other hand, makes your mouth smell like dead meat, but that
is another problem altogether.)

We are not the first to recognize this particular property of
garlic. In 1594, Thomas Nashe wrote, with great clarity and
preciseness, "Garlick makes a man winke, drinke and stinke."
He was much kinder than John Milton, however, who wrote in
1609, "The smell of Garlicke takes away the stink of dunghills."
And, we might add, gives them a whole new aroma.

One morning, while meditating on the subject of garlic, we
realized how little information we had to meditate with and decided to learn more about the peppy little critter. The best place
to do this sort of thing is the Garlic Institute of America, Inc., so
that is where we went.

The Garlic Institute of America, Inc., serves as a repository of
garlic information, garlic wisdom and garlic lore. It is financed
by the Garlic Growers Association, whose motto is "Put garlic

in your mouth," and is dedicated to expanding the use of garlic in America. The Garlic Growers are very concerned about the image of garlic, too long associated with both haute cuisine and basse cuisine but not with middle-American cooking. They also run a small publishing operation called The Garlic Press, which puts out a bimonthly, *The Repeater,* which has to do with remembrance of meals past, or, *à la recherche du repas perdu.* Basil Sage, the editor and publisher, got the idea while dunking garlic toast into cambric tea at his aunt's house one day.

When we got to the Institute, we went directly to the library and had a nice chat with Peter, the librarian. Peter told us that garlic is related to the lily family and therefore to the onion. It is also related by marriage to Nelson Rockefeller.

Garlic is apparently as old as time, if not older. It appears in the earliest literature. Peter told us that Homer mentions it. He describes how one of the gods, Hermes (who is now the patron saint of French suitcases), gave Odysseus a piece of garlic to protect him from the magic of Circe. It was called moly. After that garlic was known as holy moly.

Peter went on to quote from Hippocrates, the founding father of modern medicine and its billing practices.

"Hippocrates," he told us, "classed garlic among the sudorific (sweat-producing) drugs. He also said that garlic is hot, laxative and diuretic, but it is bad for the eyes."

"Yes," we said, "that's right. And anyone who has ever stuck a clove of garlic in his eye knows it. Other things you don't want in your eye are onions, pepper, a bowling ball and two mating black widow spiders."

"Garlic," said Peter, whose eyes had clouded over just a little, "lost its place among the pharmaceuticals during the Middle Ages."

"How come?" we asked.

"They found better medicines," he answered.

"Like what?" we asked.

"Oh, like the toad sperm, the eunuch fat, the tinctures of sow bugs and the one-a-day tablets of crocodile dung."

"How did they acquire the eunuch fat?" we asked, reaching for Valium.

Peter said he really didn't know and apologized. To change

7

the subject he explained to us about the so-called noxious odor of the moly. It seems that you eat the garlic, you digest the garlic, it enters your bloodstream and when you breathe it's expelled from your lungs in respiration. Mouth sprays are totally useless in the face of this. What is needed is a chlorophyll lung spray. Not a pretty picture. However, there is hope. If you crush or cook the garlic, the essence is released into the air before you eat it. Makes it kind of like cooking with wine, the alcohol goes and the taste remains.

We thanked Peter for all the information and time he had given us, but it was growing late and we had to leave. He pressed a small something into each our hands, and we all said goodbye. Out on the street we opened our hands and looked. There reposed small, pearly cloves of garlic. "What the hell," we said, and popped them into our mouths and chewed gaily because the truth of the matter is that true garlic-lovers don't give a good you-know-what about whether they smell or not. And you can count us among that number.

We will eat garlic in anything and have been writing to Baskin-Robbins demanding that they make a garlic ice cream. They could call it French Kiss. So far we've not heard from them, but we're keeping an eye on "the flavor of the week."

We've also devised a wonderful garlic roast entrée. You'll need about four pounds of fresh garlic for this. First peel and separate the bulbils (cloves.) Chop well, but do not bruise, until the consistency of the cloves (bulbils) is such that the entire mass can be shaped into one of the two classic forms which the garlic roast takes. One is a pillow, which is why this is called the garlic pillow roast. The other is the brick shape and is called the garlic brick roast. There is very little difference between them.

Once you've decided upon the shape of your roast, you are ready to add the seasoning, the *pièce de resistance,* which makes all the difference in this dish. Take a good sharp knife, then take an eighth of a pound of meat (lamb is best, but beef will do) and cut it into small, wedge-shaped pieces. If you leave a little fat, it will help the flavor. Now take the wedges and carefully insert them into the garlic roast and squeeze the garlic together over the meat wedges to keep the juices in. You

8

are now ready for the oven. Put your garlic roast into a lightly buttered Dutch oven. Surround it with alternating potatoes and onions. Make sure your oven is preheated to a gentle 250° and leave the garlic roast there for an hour—fifteen minutes to the pound. When it is done, you'll have a party entrée your guests will oooooh and ahhhh over—mostly oooooh.

While pursuing our exhaustive studies in menu Italian we learned that **anitra** means duck. Ibsen wrote **Peer Gynt** in Italy. The sexpot in **Peer Gynt** is named Anitra. What we're trying to figure out is, what does this tell us about Henrik Ibsen? Remember, he is also the man who gave us **The Wild Duck.**

A MAN
CALLED CARÊME,
or
LUST FOR A DISH
TO REMEMBER

We took a day off to do the fiscal thing—we paid our bills, filed our respective income taxes, and prudently made out wills, just in case we died before the refunds arrived. We also decided to donate various parts of our bodies to worthy research organizations and take the full deduction. Up until now we had been taking the standard real estate depreciation on them, but this year we gave our hearts to the heart bank, our kidneys to the kidney bank, our livers to the liver bank, our bones to the bone bank and our fat to the war effort. Besides a terrific deduction, we also got a pop-up toaster.

It was a rewarding day in more ways than one because we learned something we had never known before. Tucked inside a utility bill, in one of those newsletters designed to encourage us to save gas by using gas (sometimes called the Industrial Paradox), we were surprised to read, under the heading HE COOKED WITHOUT GAS, that classical French cuisine was created by a man named Marie Antoine Carême (1784–1833). Carême created the Charlotte Russe, Chestnut Croquettes and Veal Orloff. "Veal Orloff," it said, "was his chef d'oeuvre. Carême, the Mozart of the menu, designed this incomparable dish

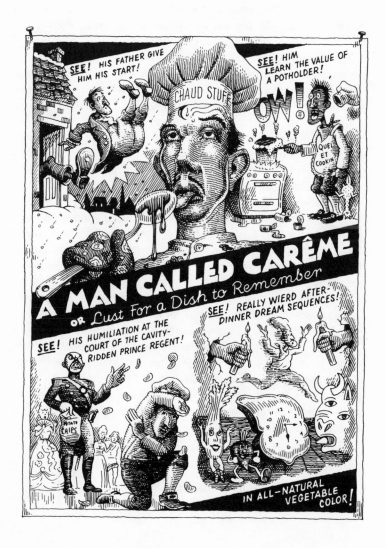

for Prince Orloff of Russia, a man who hated veal. It was the apex of a life full of artistic striving. Veal Orloff is Beethoven's Ninth, *Paradise Lost,* the Sistine Chapel, and *The Last Supper,* only edible.''

Dear God! We nearly fainted from the immensity of the idea that now hit us. No one has ever heard of this man. Beethoven, Milton, Michelangelo, yes. Carême, no.

We gazed at the little newsletter, our eyes moist, and experienced a sense of history at its most tragic. Poor Carême, passed over in the annals of time. We thought about what we—all of us—have lost because of this capricious oversight. There are no Carême Streets, no Carêmestrasses, no rues de Carême that we ever heard of. There are no Carême Festivals, no Carême shows in museums, no auctions of authenticated Carême recipes at Parke-Bernet. There are no likenesses of Carême in wax museums, no best-sellers about Carême, and Hollywood has never made the Carême movie. This is why, after two months of hard-core research, and to right this shameful wrong, we have put together *A Man Called Carême* or *Lust for a Dish to Remember,* a treatment for a screenplay to be written by us, then turned into a novel by us, then turned into a log by us, and possibly a Broadway musical by us.

In the first scene, which occurs before the credits, we dramatize the event that marked Carême for life.

The camera dollies in on the gates of an eighteenth-century French town, revealing two raggedy figures; Rachmaninoff's Variations on a Theme of Paganini is playing in the background. The raggedy figures are young Carême and his father.

The father tells the boy that business has been so bad he is going to have to let one of his twenty-five children go, and Carême is the one.

Carême looks at his father, his eyes filling with tears, his lower lip trembling.

CARÊME
But father,
if you will not provide for me,
how will I eat?

THE FATHER
Work in a restaurant, my son.
Where the chickens peck,
that's where the worm is.

CARÊME
I don't want to eat worms.

THE FATHER
Hungry children
should not be choosy.

The music swells. The camera holds on the small figure of the child slowly disappearing into the darkening streets of the town.

Now we know that all his life Carême's artistic efforts will be a tragic and desperate attempt to please a rejecting parent. (Had his father told him, "Sing for your supper," Carême might have become an opera star; had his father told him, "Beg, borrow or steal," Carême might have become the eighteenth-century equivalent of a Lockheed executive; or, had his father told him, "So starve," he might have died.)

After the credits we pick up the fledgling artist in a terrible snowstorm, alone and hungry, sucking on his sleeve, looking pitiful. He is about to meet his teacher and suffer the anguish of education. He knocks timidly at the door of a humble cookshop. The door opens, and there stands a little old, bent-over cookshop keeper, who is so old he has tufts of white hair growing out of his head.

COOKSHOP KEEPER
Come in, my boy,
I will make you a sauce.

CARÊME
(Tasting the sauce)
Have you ever thought
of using nutmeg?

Dramatic music now to underscore this moment—the first indications of genius—the bell section of Rimski-Korsakov's Russian Easter Festival Overture.

The cookshop keeper looks at the boy with new respect.

13

CARÊME
(Explaining)
My mother showed me a few
tromperies de cuisine
when I was growing up.

COOKSHOP KEEPER
How old are you now?

CARÊME
Eight.

COOKSHOP KEEPER
If I had had a boy once,
he would be your age.
Would you care to stay here
and learn to make sauces
from an old saucier?
Be my apprentice?

The boy agrees and weeps for joy.

We now envision a Slavko-Vorkapich montage of Carême making sauces under the tutelage of the old man—intense, beautifully lit, almost epic in its scope and grandeur. As musical background, the excited and neurotic part of Ravel's "Bolero."

In the montage we see Carême learn

—not to handle a knife by the
sharp side of the blade;
—the value of the pot holder;
—not to sit on a hot stove;
—not to test the fat in the
deep fryer with his finger;
—not to inhale pepper;
—that meat that smells bad should
not be eaten, except in stews.

Of course, this idyll cannot last. Carême has outgrown his teacher and has to leave him. He must learn more. We cut from the last scene of the montage to the old master at work in his kitchen clarifying butter. Several years have passed.

14

Carême enters looking older and distraught; he holds up a golden cookie covered with pieces of fried onion.

> **CARÊME**
> I have failed.
> I thought the onion cookie
> was a natural.
> In my mind's tongue
> I could taste the contrast
> of onion to cookie dough.
> Yet it came out . . .
> how can I put it . . .

> **COOKSHOP KEEPER**
> Baroque.

> **CARÊME**
> No. Neo-classical.
> You see, there is nothing
> you can teach me any more.
> Now I must explore the world
> and create something
> as good as my vision.
> I am packing my possessions
> and tomorrow I follow
> the road to discovery.

> **COOKSHOP KEEPER**
> Does this mean you are leaving?

> **CARÊME**
> Yes.

The saucier's heart breaks, and he slumps down into a lower-case "n" shape and dies.

Carême is grief-stricken and suffers intensely. He beats his head with a colander and discovers a new kind of pain—the headache.

We now take Carême, whose style has not yet jelled, into his first love affair and still more agony as he learns the terrible pain of causing pain. He goes to work in a restaurant as kitchen help. He is fifteen years old and beautiful, and he falls for Chrystal, the meat cutter's sister. She instructs young Carême in how to cut meat from the bone, to eviscerate a hen, to clean fish, to slice bacon, to chop beef and beat veal. She is his great amour and, inspired by her, he throws himself into his work.

We envision an incredible sequence in which Carême is seen working at fever pitch, lit by the volcanic heat of the oven, the sweat pouring off his body, and in his eyes the miracle spark of genius at the height of creative ecstasy. Moussorgsky's *Night on Bald Mountain* for underscoring.

Maddened, demanding more heat for a special capon, Carême burns down the kitchen. In the excitement, or perhaps because of it, he collapses and is carried to his room. At his bedside, the beautiful Chrystal sits and mops his brow with silk dipped in pure alcohol. Suddenly he comes to and throws her to one side. He rushes to the ruins of the kitchen, and with his bare hands removes the special capon. It is cooked to perfection! Holding the crisped, still-smoking eunuch chicken aloft like a trophy, Carême carries it from the burnt-out kitchen into the dining room and serves it. The diners eat everything, even the plates, and when there is no more, they carry Carême out into the streets, arrange themselves into two rows and sing, *"Je t'aime, Carême."* Carême laughs recklessly, drunk with his power to move people with his cooking.

We dissolve through this scene of triumph to Chrystal in his room, morbidly depressed, realizing that she can never compete with her lover's true mistress, Dame Kitchen. She drinks the leftover alcohol and dies. Carême is inconsolable and suffers much pain. From this point on, he looks more mature. Also his voice is deeper. He starts to shave.

Carême is now a star, and Talleyrand, the diplomat extraordinary and gourmet's gourmand, has to have Carême for his kitchen.

We see him join Talleyrand's household on the night the bananas arrive. This is a chance to glimpse a truly historical personage at home. Talleyrand, the Kissinger of his time, was very fussy about his bananas, likewise Carême, and Carême is overjoyed to watch Talleyrand grading, weighing and counting an entire shipment of Barbados bananas, carefully checking each one for imperfections. There is a lot of local color and imported color in this scene—mostly yellow because of the bananas—as all night long Talleyrand counts bananas while candles gutter and die, and Carême and the banana merchants look on.

Finally it is dawn and Talleyrand is finished. Now he welcomes Carême to his household. Carême rushes to the kitchen, eager to begin frying bananas; and the merchants leave, eager to get some sleep, which gives us an opportunity for a genuine ethnic Barbados musical number. As they stagger to their ships, the merchants spontaneously break into song.

BANANA MERCHANTS
(Singing)
Hey, Mr. Talleyrand, Tally me banana.
Daylight come and me want to go home. . . .

Carême does well in Talleyrand's kitchen. He pursues the elusive perfect recipe, and the days slip by. He is happy, but not for long. Madame de la Crêpe, the international spendthrift, is about to enter his life. Carême is about to learn the dreadful price of success.

He is called into M. Talleyrand's study one day to discuss dinner. Seated on one side of the room is the glamorous, dangerous La Crêpe, known to *tout* Paris, or *toot* Paris, if you will, as *La Belle Dame sans Merci*. As Carême enters she is bargaining with Talleyrand for one of his carriages.

LA CRÊPE
Not a cent more than
twenty-five thousand louis, Charles.
I must have that darling brougham
and those enchanting Liendenhaltzers.

Talleyrand introduces her to Carême. She tries to buy him. Talleyrand refuses. Carême leaves and returns with a napoleon.

She takes it and offers Carême fifty francs. He refuses. She offers herself. He accepts, and they have an affair.

She takes him to places he has never been: gambling halls, the stock exchange, stores that sell goods after hours. They stay up late and Madame de la Crêpe introduces him to a new crowd, the wrong crowd—shallow, well-dressed men who smile and laugh a lot but say nothing.

And wherever they go Madame de la Crêpe spends and spends and spends. In one twenty-four-hour period she buys

> –a new set of steak knives
> –matching his-and-hers sable kitchen aprons
> –a silk factory from Japan
> –September-November lobster futures
> –six hundred pounds of opium
> for the China trade
> –cast-iron models of the fifteen most
> important buildings in France
> –the Seine River
> –all the property around Notre Dame
> –one hundred and fifty Pekinese
> –everything made of ermine tails

Carême neglects his work and squanders his savings, but there is no stopping La Crêpe. After two weeks of this, he is in a state of financial ruin, and worse, his cooking has suffered. It looks like skid row for Carême, but then a representative of the Prince Regent comes over from England and invites Carême to become head cook at the Palace for twice the money he'd been getting with Talleyrand. Carême accepts. He knows this is the only way he will rid himself of La Crêpe. He breaks down when he tells Talleyrand, who forgives Carême and who blames himself for introducing them.

Alas, once at the Prince Regent's we see that life is only going to be worse for the poor foodsmith. The Prince Regent is a strong man with strong tastes who likes things to be done a certain way—his way. Carême can't stand it. He is a creative cook. He pleads with the Prince Regent.

CARÊME
All right, all right,
so I have to make
Scotch Eggs,
but please let me make them tasty.

His heartbreak is ignored. The Prince Regent keeps sending the dishes back because they are not right. In his typically understated, upper-class English fashion, he is abusive to boot.

PRINCE REGENT
(Shrieking)
Huo told you to put
goose livers on the Cornish pasties,
you froggy arse!

The words fall on Carême like blows on his back. He cries inside and develops dark hollows around his eyes.

For one of the banquets, Carême constructs a replica of Stonehenge in sugar glacé. He is appalled when guests break off pieces and dip them in marmalade. He had not anticipated the notorious English sweet tooth. He watches helplessly as the Prince Regent takes care of two uprights and a horizontal and then has the nerve to complain that the sugar glacé is too hard for his brittle, cavity-riddled teeth.

But the last straw comes when the Prince Regent humiliates Carême in front of seven hundred and fifty-eight dinner guests. (A stunning scene lit entirely by candlepower.) The Prince Regent screams at Carême.

PRINCE REGENT
You call these potatoes chips?
I call them soggy!

And he throws them at Carême one at a time. Carême just stands there and takes it, the potatoes bouncing off his chest and falling with gentle thuds on the gleaming floor. He puts up a brave front.

CARÊME
Let the chips fall where they may.

But when all the chips have fallen, Carême realizes that he cannot go on like this any longer. He musters his self-respect and tells the Prince Regent that he has had it, he is leaving.

CARÊME
I have a hunger
gnawing at my vitals,
a yearning, burning inside of me.
A need to create,
a need to cook the impossible dish,
to fry the impossible fish,
to cream the impossible cream,
to climb the highest rump roast—
and I'll never do that here!

Surprisingly, the Prince Regent gives Carême good references.

PRINCE REGENT
You were the only one hu'ose food
I could always digest.

It is obvious he does not understand why. Carême looks at him with pity.

We cut now to a snow-covered moonlit landscape in the middle of the steppes of Russia. In the background we hear "Balalaikas in the Moonlight" by the Don Cossack Chorus. A troika, pulled by three white horses—Sasha, Masha and Kasha—skims across the snow, whipped by their old driver, Glinka. In the back sits Carême, bundled up against the Russian cold. His eyes burn.

The old man lashes at the horses, who press harder against the snow. The runners on the troika make a hissing sound. Carême makes a hissing sound too. He is impatient, for he is heading for St. Petersburg and the House of Orloff, there to cook for Prince Orloff, famed patron of the edible arts. (At the last round-robin dinner of the National Academy of Edible Arts and Sciences, Orloff had been awarded the coveted Eddie for outstanding achievement in fried meat.)

Carême stands in the troika and yells to the wind.

CARÊME
I have fears
that I should cease to be
before my pots
have gleaned my teaming brain.

THE DRIVER
Sit down.
We could have an accident.

In the distance we see the lights of St. Petersburg.

To introduce himself to the Prince, and as a special treat, the next day Carême cooks his most famous speciality, *Selle de Veau Metternich,* braised saddle of veal with truffles and béchamel sauce. He slaves over it all day.

The *selle de veau* sends Orloff into a terrible rage. No sooner does he taste it than he flings it from his mouth and proceeds to break

–the dinner table
–the dishes
–the serving bowls
–the glasses
–the decanters
–the old silver samovar
–the espresso machine
–the flower vases
–the soup tureen
–the ratatouille server
–the celery holder
–the napkin rings
–the ashtrays

Cardinal Richelieu invented mayonnaise. The Four Musketeers gave us nothing.

He gets up and, raising his chair by two legs, swings it against and into the huge glass whatnot case containing his family's hereditary whatnots, including

> –a set of matching Fabergé eggs
> –gold icons of the eleventh century
> –two glass amulets containing
> bones of the saints
> –a pair of ceramic flamingos

The chair itself disintegrates under his strength.

Orloff snatches the rug from the floor and proceeds to tear it into bits, using his fingers and his teeth. He pulls down the drapes and tears them into rags. He rips the doors from their sills, splintering them with his wrath. He takes the knobs and hurls them through the windows, allowing the Russian wind to rush in, carrying with it sleet and snow. The guests, terror-stricken, flatten themselves out against what is left of the walls.

Out of breath and panting from his exertions, Orloff surveys the room. Several of the guests are sobbing, some are trying to escape over the wreckage of the doors. Orloff apologizes to them.

ORLOFF
I am a reasonable man.
It's just that I don't like veal.
I was frightened by
my mother's calf when I was a boy.

His guests forgive him.
But Carême cannot. He argues with Orloff.

CARÊME
Veal is the epicure's meat.
Beef is boring.
Pork is fatty.
And so is lamb.
But veal is divine!
It is young and innocent.
Veal comes from animals who are only

22

two and a half to three months old.
They are fed only on milk, with some eggs toward the end.
Veal is white; its fat is white,
and satiny, and smells of milk.
It is not greasy to the touch like pork.

ORLOFF
I know. I know all that.
But I don't care.
Veal makes me feel icky.

That night in bed as Carême tries to sleep, troubling images float before his eyes. Carême sees himself dancing barefoot through a fog in a diaphanous chef's suit. He hears his own voice, pushed through an echo reverberator, saying

CARÊME
How do you prepare veal for Orloff? . . .
For Orloff? . . . For Orloff? . . .

He dances past an empty chair, he dances past a dead horse, he dances past a melted cheese sandwich, which gives the time —three-thirty. This causes Carême to cry out.

Suddenly he is in a long, narrow hotel hallway flanked by many doors. The hall is lit by candles held by hands attached to human arms, which cunningly come right out of the walls. At the end of the corridor is a door which says, "Kitchen!" Carême walks through the door and finds himself falling.

He falls into Africa, where a terrible scene of pagan religious sacrifice is presented to him. Calves, carrying spears, wearing human skins and grotesque painted masks, dance in a frenzy around a large fire. On the fire is a bubbling caldron. Without warning, one of the calves breaks away from the group and dives head first into the huge pot.

He emerges from the vessel as Prince Orloff. The prince is wearing a red wig and a false nose.

ORLOFF
Guess who?

23

CARÊME
I don't get it.

ORLOFF
Disguise the veal, *imbecile-tête.*

That evening Carême serves the Prince veal stuffed into a large chicken skin. Afraid to use the word veal, he calls this dish *Stuffed Epiderma de Poulet.*
The Prince is not amused and smites the stuffed chicken skin with a wine decanter.
That night Carême picks up the dream from the night before. And in the sequel the old saucier comes running in out of the fog.

SAUCIER
Carême, here's a hint: disguise the flavor with a sauce.

He fades back into the fog, and Chrystal glides into view.

CHRYSTAL
Carême, braise the saddle
for three hours.
Remove from oven.
Carefully cut the fillets from the bones,
keeping the knife at a slant.

CARÊME
Slower, Chrystal,
I want to take notes.

CHRYSTAL
You are asleep.
If you take notes,
when you awaken
they will be nonsense.
Now to continue.
Put soubise sauce and truffles
on each slice.

Put the slices
back in the saddle again.

CARÊME
Hmmmmm, very catchy.

CHRYSTAL
Cover the entire megillah
with Mornay sauce.
Sprinkle lightly with cheese.
Brush with melted butter.
Glaze quickly in the oven.
There, that's all the hint
I'm going to give you.

She fades back into the fog.
The Orloff calf gets up from his chair and begins to pirouette.
From out of the distance, dancing *en pointe,* coming closer and
closer, are radishes, creamed cucumbers, tomato wedges, onion
slices, celery stalks and asparagus tips. It is the Corps de Garni.
The Corps dances around the Orloff calf in wider and wider
frenzies.
Carême falls out of bed.

CARÊME
(Shouting)
To work!
There's no time to be lost.
This is it!
The breakthrough of a lifetime.

Cut to the dinner. Gypsy violinists mingle among the guests,
playing "Fascination." It is a typical evening *chez* Prince Orloff,
except that tonight the Prince is in a dangerous mood, and
though he acts expansive and jolly, we see tension lines at the
corners of his eyes. Somehow he suspects Carême is going to
surprise him, and he has an idea the surprise will not be to his
liking.
In the kitchen Carême pours the last of the Mornay sauce

over the roast, gives a short prayer and sends the veal dish out
into the world.

Carême waits.

Cut to Orloff in the dining room. He samples the dish.

ORLOFF
Yagggghhhh. Aaaaaaaayahhyg.
This is tasty! What is it?

Orloff comes into the kitchen, his napkin smeared with sauce,
sauce dripping from his nose and sauce spotting his mustache
and beard.

PRINCE ORLOFF
My compliments to the chef.
I call this the perfect dish.
What do you call it?

CARÊME
I call it Veal Orloff.

Orloff staggers back, clutching his napkin.

PRINCE ORLOFF
By all that is tragic in Russia!
You've done it, Antoine.
You've made me eat veal
and like it.
I must kiss you.

CARÊME
Not on the mouth, my Prince.

PRINCE ORLOFF
Then let me celebrate
your greatness in song.

(Sings)
You're the Carême in my coffee . . .

We cut to the grand ballroom of the palace. As elegantly
dressed dancers swirl and dip in beautiful sweeping motions, the

26

camera seeks out Carême standing in the doorway in his chef's suit and tall white hat. There are tears in his eyes. He whispers to himself.

CARÊME
They think they know.
But they have never understood my work.

He is filled with anguish.

He returns to Paris, eager to work and create more, but the years in Russia have taken their toll. He coughs badly now and no one will let him near food. He passes a restaurant that features Veal Orloff and watches the diners through the window. The proprietor chases him away. Carême wanders the boulevards, ragged, unrecognized, alone and coughing. Heartbroken, he falls to the ground and rolls into the gutter and dies there.

As he passes his last breath, heavenly music swells up and his soul—through trick photography—leaves his body, and he ascends to heaven.

The film ends with Carême in heaven giving cooking lessons to the epicurean angels. As he ladles soubise sauce onto a saddle of veal, he breaks into a hacking cough. The epicurean angels hastily file out, leaving the angel Carême alone with his creation—heaven's own Veal Orloff. The heavenly choir, played by the Don Cossack Chorus, reprises "Balalaikas in the Moonlight." The artist's life, even in death, is not a happy one.

THE END

Cannibals call man the "long pig." Some reporters claim that human meat (like most exotic flesh, e.g., rattlesnake, iguana, sea cricket, etc.) tastes like chicken. But a Tahitian once said, "The white man, when well-roasted, tastes like a ripe banana."

To which we would like to add, "Only if you remember to baste every fifteen minutes."

PACK UP
YOUR TRUFFLES IN
YOUR OLD KIT BAG
AND
SMILE, SMILE SMILE

Just to add
to our knowledge

and to ground ourselves more thoroughly for the task at hand, i.e., the tasting and evaluation of good eats, your gourmand adventurers, Miss Olsen and Mr. Efron, popped into Balducci's, our neighborhood gourmet supermarket, one gloomy Sunday, and purchased a $5.45 tin of French truffles. This can was about as big as a grown man's thumb and contained three truffles—one petite and two petite-petites. We figured it out. The price per truffle was $2.7250 for the petite and $1.3625 each for the petite-petites. Now, just as any good French housewife or houseman, depending upon gender, of course (the truffles have no gender, they are fungi—a happy idea which caused us to skip home lightly singing: "In the morning, in the evening, ain't we got fungi?"—which caused the driver of a passing sanitation truck to lean out of his cab and advise us that Baygon would take care of the problem) would do, we applied some more arithmetic and discovered that our truffles would cost $99.58 a pound— a precious commodity—and hence the expression, "Worth his weight in truffles."

There they were, sitting on the plate, three of what the dictionary calls "edible blackish fruit." We feel that this is a basically correct description, but we would amend it by saying that besides being black, these truffles were knobby and strange. However, because we are intrepid and doughty, we decided to try them totally naked and in their natural state; that was so we would know, when we tasted pâté with truffles, what was the pâté and what was the truffles.

Unfortunately we couldn't determine what the taste of truffles was. Our truffles had no taste. Our $5.45 tin of truffles produced only a little grit between our teeth and, since the truffles were also so small, an empty feeling. Hence another expression: "Nobody knows the truffles we've seen." Not even us.

"But wait a minute," we asked each other. "What's going on here?" For centuries people that we like and respect have been saying wonderful things about truffles. Brillat-Savarin called truffles "the diamonds of gastronomy," which, if you think about it, makes mushrooms the zircons of gastronomy, tiny little onions the pearls, and olives the pits.

And William Makepeace Thackeray wrote in *Memorials of Gormandising*: "Presently, we were aware of an odour gradually coming towards us, something musky, fiery, savoury, mysterious, —a hot drowsy smell that lulls the senses, and yet enflames them,—the truffles were coming."

Our truffles, alas, had no smell to speak of. We sincerely wish they had. An experience as wonderful as the one Thackeray describes is well worth $5.45.

So just what is the truth about truffles? Where do they come from? Why are they so prized? We set out to find out, and we found out, and this is our report.

The ancient Greeks thought truffles were a product of thunder. In the Middle Ages truffles were considered evil things grown from the spit of witches. Wise men of the time came to this conclusion because they *knew* that the spit of witches was black and not white like that of ordinary mortals. And since truffles were black, the conclusion was obvious—to Middle-Agers, at any rate.

Later on, truffles became revered as an aphrodisiac, and Madame de Pompadour fed them to Louis XV. And Marie Antoinette fed them to Louis XVI. But then the French populace rose up, so nobody knew if they worked or not.

Napoleon, on the other hand, was sure that they worked. He was having trouble fathering children and begat his only son after eating a truffled turkey.ˋ This thrilled him so much that he promoted a lieutenant to colonel for having given him the recipe. We understand that the colonel was an incompetent and contributed greatly to the debacle in Russia and so, so much for the truffled colonel, who proved to be a turkey, and for the role of truffles in history.

There is one truly wonderful feature of the truffle and that is that it grows underground around the roots of certain oak trees and is therefore very difficult to detect. This makes the truffle a genuine subterranean savory. And gives us yet another memorable expression: "From the humble oak the mighty truffle grows."

There are several ways to find truffles: Sometimes they make cracks in the earth as they grow, and with a lot of practice you can learn to spot them. Many species of flies live on truffles (flies are never ones to pass up dainties—this is characteristic of vermin) and, in the morning and evening, columns of small yellow flies may be seen hovering over a colony, hoping that you will come along and dig them up. But the mainstream of truffle gatherers prefers to hunt the truffle with the aid of a pig. Since *most* truffles are found in France and only *some* truffles are found in Northern Italy, the odds are that the pig used most often is a French pig.

The grandeur of the following procedure is typical of the French. There is the right way of doing things and then there is the French way, which is always better. What a Frenchman does may seem arbitrary, but there is a banal logic behind it, known throughout the departments of France as *La Grande Logique,* or *La Banalité Perfecte.*

Most of these *banalités* begin at 4:30 in the morning when the French farmer awakens his hunting sow and puts all 450 pounds of her into the back seat of his Citroën Deux Chevaux. As soon as she is comfortable they drive to where the oak trees are. When they get there, the farmer tenderly helps his heavy

porker from the car and into the wheelbarrow, which he has removed from the trunk for just this purpose. The farmer now wheels his companion toward the woods, where they hope to connect with a truffle bed. After he takes the pig out of the wheelbarrow, he attaches a cord to one of the pig's back legs, and they are off and running at the hunt.

This is where the highly developed porcine olfactories of the sow come into play as, snout to ground, she snuffles and snorts her way closer to the elusive earth-nut. Suddenly her snorts become excited grunts, her body stiffens, the bristles on her back begin to quiver. We read that a trained hog, when she has discovered a truffle bed, is immovable. As far as we're concerned, a 450-pound pig is at all times immovable, but apparently not to the truffle-hunting French farmer. As soon as the pig points, the farmer tugs quickly at the cord and manages to pull her back before she can reach the truffle and eat it.

Now comes the most desperately sensitive part of the hunt, the *instant critique* (critical instant). The farmer must prevent his pig from eating the delectable "gastronomical diamond" without discouraging her to the point where she will not go on to find more truffles. So he runs around to the front of the animal and offers her an acorn, which she takes. While she is occupied with the acorn, he gets down and digs up the truffle himself. All of which goes to prove that oinkers may have a keen sense of smell but not much of any other kind of sense. They are noted for making bad bargains, and the evidence is that they will trade a truffle for an acorn—thus making the acorn a bridge over truffled barters.

The French have pigs to help them in their search for truffles, but the proud Arab elects to do his truffle snorting or rooting for himself. (Whereas the best truffles come from the Perigord region of France and other quite good truffles grow in Italy, there is another truffle that grows just beneath the surface of the Sahara sands and the bedouins are mad for them.) These wandering traders have learned from centuries of experience that their camels are of no particular use in stalking the desert passion-clod. You can lead a camel to truffles, but you can't make him snort. Therefore, the bedouins use their own keen sense of sight. In the early morning or late afternoon, the slanted rays of the sun cause shadows to lengthen at the base of the small mounds the truffles push up. The truffle-crazed sons of Allah look for truffle shadows and pounce with glee upon the mounds. "Truffles, Ya Ha!"

They roast them at night in the hot ashes of their campfire, dip them in salt and eat them under the desert stars. What they don't eat they take with them. They don't give any to their camels—who don't deserve them anyway.

Certain people, profit-hungry delicatessen owners and proprietors of gourmet shops in New York City, have asked the question "What about the efficacy of importing French pigs to the Sahara desert as aids in the never-ending search for truffles?" And the answer to that is, "Arabs are quite finicky about pigs." For one thing they are not very keen on pork. They don't admire the pig and will tell you that pigs are a nuisance on a caravan. If they carried pigs they would have to stop at every oasis along the way to let them wallow in the mud holes. After that, who would want to drink the water? If the pigs were not allowed to wallow, they would grunt and complain because their complexions would be baked and dried by the sun. So what we have is a real problem. French pigs don't like the desert and the desert doesn't like French pigs.

At this point all our research added up to one indisputable fact—people everywhere were hot for truffles, and this did not gibe with our truffle experience. We were wondering how we were going to explain this discrepancy, when a parking-lot attendant told us that canned truffles often have no taste and are sometimes even dyed black to boot. So that was it! We had had canned, tasteless truffles and had allowed that to flavor our opinion. Maybe we should have cooked them.

There is, we have decided, only one way out. The French way. We will have to go to Perigord and get our truffles straight from the horse's mouth, or, in this case, the pig's. We are saving pennies now. There is even a Cro Magnon Hotel in the region (also famous for caves of the same name) which conjures up fascinating pictures in our minds of fascinating service and fascinating cooking methods.

Because we read in Brillat-Savarin's book that a truffled turkey was a luxurious item which could be seen only on the tables of the highest nobility and the best-paid whores, we intend to begin our true truffle adventures with a turkey stuffed with truffles.

And who knows what this will lead to? The motto of any true truffle fanatic is: Find an opening and stuff it—Life Savers, doughnuts, bagels—the list is endless, but hang the expense, Gridley, we have but one tongue.

WINE

ON

LINE

Wednesday

morning is our

morning to visit the unemployment office. There are times when
even such as we must give up the world of the bejeweled and
the monied and go each week to sign for our stipends and, more
important, to embrace the cloak of democracy and join the common run with the real people who speak the real argot of reality
as it is perceived in the real city. To give you some idea of
the tone of the place let us tell you that there is a sign Scotch-
taped to the door which reads, "No Radio Playing." (This raises
the unemployment office several cuts above The Pride Center on
New York City's Lower East Side, which bears the international
sign for no-guns-allowed on the door—a picture of a revolver
with a diagonal line canceling it out.)

During our last claim (since we work together, we are nearly
almost always unemployed together) we got to know some of
our fellow unemployables and, because we were lucky enough
to collect for the entire twenty-six weeks plus two thirteen-week
extensions, we got to regret having made the acquaintance of
Mr. Horvath, the clockmaker with the hair-trigger temper; Gordon
You-there-stand-in-line Dunne, the Official Volunteer Monitor of
the World; Mrs. Smalk, the woman who gets people to do things
for her: "Could you hold my place in line, please? Could you

pass the Living Section of your *Times* since you're not reading it? May I borrow your comb?'' She is also a Cancer and proud of it. And Arturo, the Hispanic pencil-tapper, who has a portable radio locked inside his skull that no one can hear but him, and he's grooving, *babeeee*, it's Salsa all the way. If he couldn't tap his pencil, he'd click his teeth in time to his music. One morning he actually scraped his pencil in rhythm against the zipper of his fly.

But some days it's worth it. Some days our faith in humanity is restored. Some days we listen to others and learn something, and those days we cherish and remember for the rest of our lives. The day of the wine chat was just such an event.

We'd been standing there noticing how we'd chosen the wrong line again—the other four lines were all moving but ours had maintained the status quo for fifteen minutes already—when the subject of *basse cuisine* came up, perhaps because we were hungry or possibly because the Sabrett's hot-dog man came in to make a delivery—two franks, one with mustard, one with mustard and onions, and two Yoo-Hoos. After the subject of *basse cuisine* came up it was a quick stumble to the wine question.

"What wine," we wondered, "do you drink when you're eating *basse cuisine*? What wine brings out the subtle, almost narcotic taste of the potato fried in grease? And what wine blends harmonically with its delicate, crisp outer crust to inspire the velvety white inner meat to yield up its ultimate flavor? What," we asked, "are the correct wines for the Big Boy, the Whopper, the Blimpie, the Hero, the Hoagie, the Submarine and the Kentucky Colonel (both regular and extra-crispy)? And what about the Souvla King? The Dairy Queen? *And* the White Castle?"

"I couldn't help overhearing you," said Mr. Modean, the man in the polyester double-knit leisure suit, who is anxious to let the bureaucrats on the other side of the counter know that his unemployed state is merely a temporary condition—he is really not one of us. "And the answer to that, if you'll allow me, is quite simple. Fast foods are designed for rapid service and they demand quick wines, *bas vins,* wines aged on their way to you in the back of the truck. As they say in the industry, 'The wine forms in the rear.' "

"You tell 'em, Windy," said Gregory, the black man two places

35

ahead of us in line. "I wish this line would move, man, I got to get back to work."

Having settled the question of what kind of wine to drink, we were immediately struck with another: "How does one recognize a good *bas vin* when one sees one?"

Gregory knew. "The answer to that one is actually quite complex," he told us. "For one thing, since this kind of wine is *mis en bouteille en fabrique,* the first thing you want to look for is a metal screw-off top or a plastic cork. Can you dig on that?"

"Also," said Mrs. Smalk, "a genuine *bas vin* looks good in a brown paper bag, so you can drink it neat-on-the-street or bring it with you into any fast-food establishment you care to patronize and surreptitiously take a swig without the manager's noticing you." She gave Arturo a meaningful look. He gave his pants a little hitch and composed his face to look handsome and macho.

Gregory continued nonplussed, "Price can also be a good indicator. None of these wines costs more than a dollar ninety-eight. Many of them are even cheaper."

"But don't be put off by an expensive bottle," interjected Mr. Horvath with a sneer. "Remember the quality can be just as *bas* as in a cheap bottle."

"A suitable *bas vin* will bear a good *American* name," declared Mr. Modean suddenly. "Names like Ripple, Zapple, Eden Roc, Key Largo, Boone's Farm and Italian Swiss Colony."

"And don't forget Mad Dog 20-20," said Gregory. "Pure American with none of your Continental overtones."

"Mad Dog 20-20?" we asked. "Does that mean it improves your vision or your bite?"

"Neither," said Gregory, "but it does improve the way you see things." He bopped a little for our benefit.

"M-D 20-20 is the real name," said Mrs. Smalk, now eyeing Gregory with a suspicious look. "M-D stands for Mogen David."

"Hey, man," said Arturo, "All those wines, man, you cannot go wrong. And, hey dig, they got new flavors all the time, man, coming out. Keep an open mouth on the subject. Like I know Gregory over here, my main man, is waiting for the Gallo Brothers, Frank and Jesse, to bring out Watermelon Wine."

Gregory laughed and said, "And you're waiting for the wine

36

made from the official bird of Puerto Rico—Fly Wine.''

We entered into the spirit of things. ''We are eagerly antici-
pating the advent of Diet Beaujolais, Lo-Cal Burgundy, Fat-Free
(no animal fats added) Chablis, Polyunsaturated Sauternes and
Weight-Watcher's Liebfraumilch. And also, something for which
there really is no real need, and which is not, strictly speaking
a wine: Decaffeinated Instant Irish Coffee with whipped Pream
and artificial sweetener.''

''Oh yeah,'' said Arturo, bobbing his shoulders in three-quar-
ter time, ''how about Brillo juice?''

A cheer went up from the line, not because of the exquisite
thoughts just expressed but because the line had moved; two
clients had been processed quickly.

We shuffled up two places and then addressed the group.
''Now we know how to recognize a *bas vin,* but how do we
know what *bas vin* goes with what *basse produit comestible*?''

The uniformed guard came over to our group, pointed a finger
at us and said sternly, ''Watch your tongues, you two. We don't
like that kind of talk in here. This is the State of New York.''

''Screw the State of New York,'' shouted several people in the
next line over.

The uniformed guard left us to attend to a fellow who was
lighting up under the No Smoking sign. ''They come in here off
the street just to smoke illegally,'' he said.

''Look at it this way,'' said Gregory, ignoring the screw altogether. ''The accepted rule, red wine with meat, white wine
with fish or poultry, is out of the question in this category. Like
the color of the wine bears no relation to the taste, you dig? The
high sugar content takes care of that. So, the only thing you can
do is to let the color of your threads be your guide. White wine
with light-color clothes to disguise any spillage, and red with
dark clothes for exactly the same reason.''

''What about cellaring the *bas vin*?''

''Don't,'' he answered. ''*Bas vins* are best stored in the chan-
delier or tied to a string and hung out a window.''

''You're not giving the complete picture,'' said Mr. Modean
suddenly from behind his *Wall Street Journal.* ''Take-out is a
major new development of the fast-food industry and with it has
come a whole new leisure-time activity—eating at home. That

37

brings up a brand new set of problems. Anyone giving an elegant dinner party—lush Les Baxter on the Hi-Fi, a couple of aromatic candles flickering on the mantel, a platter of Arthur Treacher's Fish and Chips, a Shakey's pizza or a stack of IHOP pancakes on the table, and a well-chosen bottle of *bas vin* cooling in the ice bucket—will want to know the special requirements for properly tasting and serving *bas vin:* the Rules of *Bas Vin* Etiquette."

Just at this moment, the line moved again and Gregory's turn came. We all watched with interest because Gregory's claim appeared to be in jeopardy. The clerk had some extra papers for him and, after looking at them for five minutes and conferring with two colleagues for ten, the supervisor was called in and poor Gregory was ordered to go to line C and wait—line C, the great Sargasso Sea of Claimants—line C, where it takes so long to be called that you have to sit down and wait instead of standing—line C, where men grow old and women don't look any better for the experience. Gregory shook hands down the line and everyone wished him well. "Sometimes your number comes up and you got to play it all the way out," he said.

"So long, sucker," said Arturo. "I'm going to miss you." They embraced. And Gregory sauntered off, playing it cool.

"Next," said the clerk. Mrs. Smalk stepped up to the counter. "I didn't get my check last week," she said. "Could you see if it was sent? Oh, I didn't bring my book, but I can tell you my number, if you give me a minute. I have such a headache, do you think you could spare an aspirin? I need a pen. Are these all the pencils you have?"

The clerk had opened the drawer at her side and was taking things out. She produced a pen, a bottle of aspirin and several forms.

"Do you have a paper cup?" asked Mrs. Smalk. "I'll have to drink some water with the aspirin."

The clerk, who has seen 'em come and seen 'em go and who wished they would all go, bit the bullet and prepared to deal with this somehow. "You'll pass the water fountain on the way out," she said. "But before you leave, answer my questions, please. Did you work last week? And were you willing, ready, and able to work? Did you move during the week?" Mrs. Smalk tried to remember. The rest of us turned our attention

38

to the unresolved questions of *bas vin* etiquette.

It was Arturo who was most helpful. "Do it nice, do it right and be cool, dig?" He stepped out of line, executed two short steps, a long step to the side, clapped his hands, turned neatly on his toes and rejoined us.

"Like how?" we asked.

"Like rule number one," he said. "To make the taste buds receptive to the flavor-jolt of the *bas vin,* cleanse and stimulate your palate by chewing several sticks of gum at once—preferably Dentyne." He snapped his fingers. "Rule number two: As soon as you open the bottle, what they call on the street the moment of *de-cappé,* drink the wine fast, 'cause if you let it breathe it will take all the oxygen out of the room. Rule number three: If it is being passed around, it is considered bad form to chug the whole bottle—don't Bogart the Bot, you dig, man? Rule four: When three or four bottles are going, clinking bottles is very bourgeois. You don't wanna do it." He took out his comb and beat out the rhythms of "Perdido" on his head.

We thanked Arturo, said we'd never forget the four cardinal rules—or him, for that matter—and, one at a time, stepped up to the counter and answered the ritual questions: "Did you work last week?"

"No."

"Were you ready, willing and able to work?"

"Yes."

"Did you turn down any jobs?"

"No."

"Did you change your address?"

"No."

"Are you in school?"

"No."

Having given the ritual responses, we signed for another payment. On the way out we waved to Gregory in the C section. Gregory held up a bottle of Richard's Wild Irish Rose, pointed to it and saluted us. We noted that he'd made the right choice— Richard's Wild Irish Rose is red. So was Gregory's shirt.

After lunch (Arthur Treacher's Fish and Chips/Boone's Farm Country Kwencher), we put together the following charts, which we sincerely hope will be helpful.

BASSE CUISINE-BAS VIN SELECTOR CHART

Incomplete Guide to What to Drink while Eating

The left-hand column lists *basse cuisine* foods. The top line lists *bas vins* Brands. A check mark (✔) in the appropriate box indicates acceptable wine. No check mark ( ) indicates that wine and food are incompatible.

TEAR OUT

TEAR OUT

	RIPPLE	EDEN ROC	ZAPPLE	KEY LARGO	BOONE'S	ITALIAN SWISS COLONY	SANT' GRIA	ORANGE/PAPAYA FLAVORED BALI HAI	ALL OTHERS
BIG MAC	✔	✔	✔	✔	✔	✔	✔	✔	✔
BIG BOY	✔	✔	✔	✔	✔	✔	✔	✔	✔
WHOPPER	✔	✔	✔	✔	✔	✔	✔	✔	✔
FILET-O-FISH	✔	✔	✔	✔	✔	✔	✔	✔	✔
BLIMPIE	✔	✔	✔	✔	✔	✔	✔	✔	✔
HERO	✔	✔	✔	✔	✔	✔	✔	✔	✔
HOAGIE	✔	✔	✔	✔	✔	✔	✔	✔	✔
SUBMARINE	✔	✔	✔	✔	✔	✔	✔	✔	✔
KENTUCKY COLONEL	✔	✔	✔	✔	✔	✔	✔	✔	✔
KENTUCKY COLONEL (BARBEQUE)	✔	✔	✔	✔	✔	✔	✔	✔	✔
SOUVLAKI	✔	✔	✔	✔	✔	✔	✔	✔	✔
ALL OTHERS	✔	✔	✔	✔	✔	✔	✔	✔	✔

BAS VIN SELECTOR CHART

Complete Guide to What to
Drink while Eating and Wearing Clothes

The left-hand column lists *bas vins*. The top line lists light-and-dark-clothing choices plus fabric selector.

	LIGHT	DARK	COTTON	WOOL	POLYESTER DOUBLE KNIT
RICHARD'S WILD IRISH ROSE		✔	✔	✔	
NIGHT TRAIN		✔	✔		
MAD DOG (MOGEN DAVID) 20–20		✔			✔
ANNIE GREENSPRINGS (ORANGE SATIN)	✔		✔		
THUNDERBIRD		✔			✔
BOONE'S FARM APPLE	✔		✔		
" " WILD MOUNTAIN		✔	✔	✔	✔
" " STRAWBERRY HILL	✔	✔	✔	✔	✔
" " COUNTRY KWENCHER	✔		✔	✔	✔
SWISS-UP	✔			✔	
MARDI GRAS PINEAPPLE WINE	✔				✔
RIPPLE	✔		✔		✔
EDEN ROC	✔		✔	✔	
ZAPPLE	✔		✔	✔	
KEY LARGO	✔				✔
ITALIAN SWISS COLONY	✔	✔	✔		✔
SANT' GRIA		✔			✔
BALI HAI	✔	✔	✔	✔	✔
ALL OTHERS	✔	✔	✔	✔	✔

TEAR OUT

TEAR OUT

41

DRINKING TOO MUCH WINE,
or
THE HANGOVER:
WHAT TO EAT,
WHAT TO WEAR,
AND WHEN NOT TO MOVE

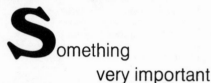

Something very important that we have discovered about the taste of wine is that the first bottle is good, the second bottle is excellent and the third bottle is sublime. We have also discovered that after the third bottle, most people feel dizzy; their eyes droop asymmetrically, so that one eye is half open and the other mostly closed. Also, the things they say don't come out sensibly. Sometimes people say things like, "This roast is salad!" or "Man the lifeboats!"

Many are given to indiscreet behavior. A friend of ours, Dorian Treadway, is frequently given to riddles. It also happens that sometimes the riddles don't come out right and once at a formal dinner for eighty-six he asked Wally Simpson, "What weighs four thousand pounds, is blue, flies, has four wings and is black and white and red all over?"

Mrs. Simpson, a well-mannered woman, said, "I don't know. What?"

Dorian answered, "A pair of four-thousand-pound garbage trucks," and laughed from the sheer pleasure of it all.

The Duke, who was alive then, leaned over and asked, "What is this about garbage trucks?"

Mrs. Simpson said, "A pair of them, dear, at two thousand pounds."

"I would think that's quite right," said the ex-monarch.

Dorian, now feeling supremely confident, asked, "How do you keep a fish from smelling?"

This time it was the Duke who entreated, "I don't know. How do you keep a fish from smelling?"

Dorian answered brightly, with a look that said what-a-good-boy-am-I, "You cut off his nose."

"How ghastly," said the Duchess. "Come, Edward, we have to leave now."

And they left, thus spoiling the party for everyone.

Never being invited back is not the only price one pays for one's spiritual pleasures. The morning after Mr. Treadway's evening out was much worse than his night before. Mr. Treadway awoke at mid-morning in much pain and discomfort. He invited death to come and relieve him.

Many people feel this way the next morning after a night out and that is because they are suffering from a hangover, which is sometimes known as consumer's remorse, imbiber's blues, tippler's tragedy or the curse of the living dead. It is not to be confused with the *faux* hangover, which could be any old headache (migraine, concussion, percussion, etc.), or merely an attack of *ptomaine morbus*. The following set of criteria should be helpful in determining the *vrai* hangover from the *faux* hangover. You have a *vrai* hangover if

1

You get up in the morning and crash to the floor
and lie there not moving for several minutes.
(You may have a hangover
or you may have broken your spine
in your sleep and, if this is the case,
you will not be able to wiggle your toes).

2

You go to the bathroom and discover that you left
your head in the other room, and you wish you hadn't.

3

You notice a new sensitivity to air currents, and
the sound of the curtains hanging is driving you crazy.

43

4

Each eyeball weighs five pounds in its socket and
is rapidly gaining weight.

5

The inside of your mouth
tastes like the floor of the bus,
and smells like the exhaust;
and all the perfumes of Arabia
and all the mouthwashes of the U.S. of Avia
cannot savia.

6

Saint James the Dismembered
comes to you in a visitation
and tells you he is
the Patron Saint of Hangovers.

Should any or all of the above apply to you, you qualify. Congratulations.

Once you've acquired a hangover, you might want to get rid of it, and that brings us to the cure. The hangover cure, by the way, is as old as alchemy, and ever since its beginnings (a tumbler full of boiling lead first thing in the morning), it has provoked controversy. Everyone has his favorite remedy. If, in the upcoming list, we have left out yours, please forgive us.

1

Some experts suggest taking charcoal tablets
to absorb the impurities and toxic substances
from your stomach.
In an emergency you might munch a briquet
from the backyard barbecue,
and we recommend a shot of naphtha
to go along with it.
But watch out for the shock wave afterwards.
It's a dilly.

2

The Hollywood-movie-best-friend-
butler-and/or-friendly-bartender remedy:

ST·JAMES THE DISMEMBERED· PATRON SAINT OF HANGOVERS

Start with a glass of tomato juice,
add Worcestershire sauce, A-1 Sauce,
jalapeño peppers, a raw egg,
chopped onion, the juice of a lemon,
the juice of a clam, croutons,
grated Parmesan cheese,
oil of wintergreen and Karo syrup.
Add salt and pepper to taste and
give to your best friend, butler and/or bartender.

3
Take two aspirin, then take morphine,
codeine, Demerol, nitric oxide,
cocaine, acid, several buds of peyote;
go to bed, pull up the covers and wait.

4
For a quick eye-opener
add four or five drops of Tabasco sauce
to your Visine.

5
Cover your head with short pieces of Scotch Tape.
Band-Aid is also good.

About what to wear for a hangover. Try to wear loose, comfortable clothing. There's no sense trying to look your best when you don't feel it. On the other hand, if the hangover is very severe and you think you might die, try to look sharp. Put on your finest evening wear and accessories, shine your shoes, stretch out on the bed and wait. If the reaper comes, you'll make a great impression. If he doesn't, you can change into something more casual and not tell anyone.

And finally, about not moving. If you can't, don't.

Epics describe the brave deeds of men called epicures. They are sometimes written in the heroic cutlet.

AL AND LOU'S
HAWAIIAN DELIGHT
LUAU PIT

The Beautiful
People (BP),
according to
WWD, Town and Country, Charlotte Curtis, Suzy and Dear Abby,
have discovered a new fun restaurant. Everybody says they don't
go there for the food, it's the atmosphere they love and the fact
that they get to see all their friends: Lee Radziwill, Marion
Javits, Andy Warhol, Bianca Jagger, Diana Vreeland, Margaret
Trudeau, Kevin McCarthy, Eric Hoffer. You name them, if they've
been in the papers, they've been to the Pit, Al and Lou's Hawaiian Delight Luau Pit. If you've not been there, you're nobody.
It's a must. *And* this place is considered to be a total gas.

Since we don't like to be left out of anything pertaining to
the high life, we hurried over to be among the first to appreciate
Al and Lou's before it got ruined and the wrong people started
going there. As we always say, "When they've let us into a
place, you know it's the beginning of the end. *Après nous, le
déluge.*" And as a matter of fact, as soon as we walked in we
heard someone say, "Uh oh, there's Olsen and Efron, this is
the beginning of the end. *Après eux, le déluge.*"

The restaurant has a Hawaiian motif. That's because the jet

set travels a lot—South America, the Sahara, Tahiti—by jet, of course, and they've developed a taste for exotic atmosphere that can't be stopped. They also suffer from chronic jet lag. You know, up in the morning and right back to bed. But that's neither here nor there. And that's where they are, neither here nor there.

Looking around we noticed that the restaurant was full of people, the talk was loud—laughter, drinking and eating going on like you wouldn't believe. We asked Al Perlbergers, the owner and a man considered a total gas by almost everyone, to explain this.

"Our food," he said, "is not exactly authentic Hawaiian, but it is carefully prepared to please our clientele."

"And who are they?" we asked.

"Pigs," he replied blandly and walked away.

That stymied us for a while and we took to studying the waiters—old men in Hawaiian grass skirts, barefooted and without shirts. Some of them we remembered from the late and much lamented Ratner's Dairy Restaurant on Second Avenue in New York's historic Lower East Side—good old Victor and good old Leo.

"Hello, Victor," we said, recognizing our favorite old waiter despite his grass skirt and lei.

"Drop dead, but don't do it here," said Victor, making us feel right at home.

We could hardly hear ourselves talk, not only because of the total commitment to Don Ho in the juke box, but also because of the noisy decor. Now, let us explain this. This room was designed to give you a compressed conception of Hawaii. Every fifteen minutes by the clock, the volcano, Mauna Loa, erupts behind the glass window on the west wall, spewing streams of red lava, portions of rock and steam—all accompanied by appropriate sound effects. The east wall is a real tropical treat, a genuine South Seas monsoon behind glass. However, in order to keep it from becoming too sterile, live mosquitos are let into the room simultaneously. This happens every ten minutes.

Al is proudest of his authentic earthquake effect, which shakes the room and is accompanied by a terrific low rumbling sound.

We asked what the timing was on this and Al answered, "Whenever the subway passes underneath."

Every now and then, these effects get into sync and they all go off at once. The customers love it, but the monkeys really hate it. They live in the papier-mâché coconut trees that dot the room, the fronds of which bend over the tables like garden umbrellas. The monkeys like to watch the people eat. We got very attached to ours till he dropped a few coconuts and beaned us on our noggins.

Finally, we got around to sampling the food. Sometimes you forget that that's why you're there. Anyway, sample we did. We didn't finish anything on the plate. They had one dish called

Pearl Harbor ($7.95); it's an appetizer—imitation poi on burnt toast. It tasted like grease thickened with corn starch and too much MSG. We asked Al Perlbergers to explain this dish to us. He said, "Nothing gets wasted around here." We figure it's called Pearl Harbor because it gives you a surprise attack Sunday morning.

For an entrée Miss Olsen had Turkey Wahini—turkey steamed in its original feathers and stuffed with sugar. The head is left on as a special delicacy. It costs $13.50 and comes with peas, carrots and mashed potatoes.

Mr. Efron had Haloki Aku-Aku, which is diced turtle meat in the shell with a side of dyed turtle eggs and jelly beans. It cost $25.00, and he says, "It dried my mouth up so I couldn't spit."

Miss Olsen couldn't tell you how the turkey tasted. She didn't even try it. Looking around the room, we noticed that Ringo Starr was delicately plucking his turkey and dropping the feathers on the floor. He appeared to be in a state of high anguish.

Alexander Haig was there in full uniform as Kommandant-Marshal of NATO, and he seemed pleased with his plate of Wakka-Wakka-Wahu. We asked Al Perlbergers what was in the Wakka-Wakka-Wahu.

"It's a famous Hawaiian peasant dish," he advised us, "made traditionally from leftovers and highly spiced with milk from the rubber tree. What General Haig is eating is basically orange peels, cantaloupe rinds, fish heads and egg shells on a bed of coffee grounds. It costs $75.00 for two, and you have to give us a day or two to make it."

So much for the entrées. For dessert we both had the cheesecake. It was made with donkey's milk, but we wondered if it wasn't milk of magnesia. Al denied everything. He's very smooth. But that's what it takes to be a high-class host, what did we expect?

As we left, we noticed that our monkey had come down and was finishing our food. We hope he's all right.

MUTTON
JEFF

When we read
that Lizzie Borden
ate cold mutton soup for breakfast on the day she "took an ax
and gave her father forty whacks, and when she saw what she
had done, she gave her mother forty-one," we knew that this
was the dish that dreams are made of, and planned a mutton
dinner.

Mutton is a meat that neither of us had ever eaten, and as we
scoured the city trying to buy a good-sized mutton roast we discovered that sheep meat is very hard to come by and that it is
a universal topic—everybody has an opinion and nobody knows
what they're talking about.

An old buddy, Rick, the Indian from the Bronx, told us that
mutton has a wool-grease taste and the way to get rid of it is
to baste the meat with cold coffee.

The man in Bobel Brothers' Butchery—the pleasant one, the
one with the cleaver scars on his nose, the one who's willing to
lower himself and talk to the customers—said, "You're out of
your minds."

An old Jewish man on the subway told us, "Mutton is a lot like
fish. You can get it at Sheepshead Bay."

"A lot like fish?" we asked. "How is it a lot like fish?" But the old man had reached his stop. He got off and we rolled on.

Sheepshead Bay is in Brooklyn, and you can get fish there. You can even go fishing from there. But you cannot get mutton there. You can get mutton at Ottomanelli's Meat Market on Bleecker Street in Greenwich Village, and, ironically, there is a sheep's head in the window. Perhaps the old man was talking in code. Alas, we'll never know.

The age of ripeness begins when the lamb becomes a mutton—on its first birthday. The sheep of one year is yesterday's lamb, today's mutton and tomorrow's dinner. At Ottomanelli's they age it a little, then freeze it. A gracious and charming Italian butcher in a blood-smeared apron told us to marinate it, as it thawed, in olive oil and wine with a nice bay leaf and some garlic, and then roast it and baste it with the marinade, which is what we did. It was going to be a Mediterranean mutton as opposed to mutton prepared by Ye Olde Englishe Methode, which involves plunging the mutton into boiling water and leaving it there for a long time, while quaffing great drafts of ale and dancing in the kitchen to the accompaniment of fiddles and lots of laughter.

We didn't do any of those exciting things while waiting for our mutton to roast—and shrink. By the way, it has a strong tendency to do that. We just sat quietly in the kitchen, listening to the wine breathe, and chatting about this and that. We'd been seeing a lot of books and articles devoted to the art of relaxation, articles that told us "How to Take a Fifteen-Minute Vacation Every Day," and books that stress the importance of shutting out the practical world of problem-solving and competition, and we had to admit, with a sigh of regret, that this was not our problem. Our problem is that we suffer from too much relaxation and just can't stop. In fact, sometimes a fifteen-minute relaxation vacation turns into a three- or four-hour holiday. We live in constant dread of having relaxation creep up on us, catching us unawares and putting us to sleep completely. This is also true of our friends and lovers. And we have reason to believe that there are even more of us than one might imagine. Therefore we would like to volunteer a few helpful hints on keeping tense and living longer.

1
Immediately upon arising,
think disturbing thoughts and keep it up all day.

2
Say unpleasant things to people.

3
When you get in an airplane,
sit backwards.

4
When you make or do anything,
be sure it's perfect!

5
Tell everyone around you that you are all right.
Do it often.
This will make them tense too.

6
When you get home in the evening,
play your television and radio as loud as you can
and try not to listen to either of them.

7
When your neighbors telephone,
tell them you are all right
no matter what they say.

Edible underpants are now available from Fredericks of Hollywood. You can eat them or wear them, or both. They come in four flavors and colors: Banana Delight (yellow), Passion Fruit (orange), Peppermint (green) or Hot Cherry (red). And one size fits all.

` The Candy Pants, as they are called, come in two sexes. For him: brief. For her: bra and bikini.

Fredericks claims that unlike all other underwear, Candy Pants improve with body heat and moisture.

Why pack a lunch? Wear your meal to work. Invite friends. When you say "The lunch is on me," you'll mean it.

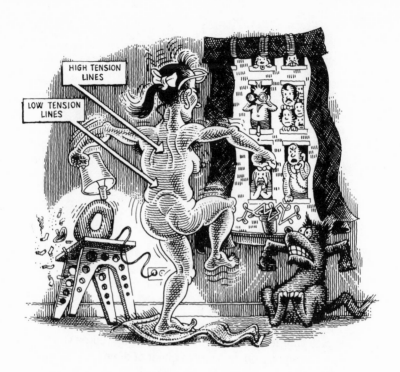

And now for our recommended ultimate tension exercise. You can do it in your own home. Here it is.

Take off all your clothing and sit by an open window. Raise your arms and moan loudly. Hold this position until everyone in the building next door is watching you. Then grab your feet with your hands and rock back and forth while singing "This Is My Country." Stand up and hop on one foot with your arms outstretched. You have no idea how tense this will make you and how tense it will make your neighbors.

And now—how did our mutton come out? Well, it was delicious. We christened it Mutton Jeff and then ate of it till there was nuthin' lef'. This is a much maligned meat. The victim of a lot of unnecessary derogation. It is not lamb, but it is like lamb except that it has more taste. It is mature lamb, adult lamb, R-rated lamb. However, we must tell you, it is expensive and it doesn't exactly melt in your mouth. It sits there and you chew and you chew and you chew—which is not bad because you exercise and eat at the same time. Why, you might burn up three or four calories that way and every little bit helps.

Would we eat it again? Yes, we would. But lamb is better. And maybe that is why mutton is hard to come by and lamb is not.

We were reading in **The Golden Bough** (just for fun) and came across this interesting comment, "The savage commonly believes that by eating the flesh of an animal or man he acquires not only the physical, but even the moral and intellectual qualities which were characteristic of that animal or man." Sir James George Frazer then gives us some examples. He tells us that "The Caribs abstained from the flesh of the pig lest it should cause them to have small eyes like pigs; and they refused to partake of tortoises from a fear that if they did so they would become heavy and stupid like the animal." Later he tells us, "When a Wagogo man of East Africa kills a lion, he eats the heart in order to become brave like a lion; but he thinks that to eat the heart of a hen would make him timid." Sir James goes on like this for several pages more. People are eating kangaroos, tigers, hearts of wolves, tongues of birds, ants and, inevitably, an enemy killed in battle—but only if he was brave.

Of course, these people are savages, but what if they are right? We like to keep an open mind. Will overindulgence in too much turkey meat make us turkey-witted? If we eat too much pork, will we have cravings for mud? What about crabs? Will we want to walk sideways? Or sheep's brains? Have we eaten too much chicken liver and does that account for a certain craven attitude toward life, or does it explain our tendency to hysterical overreacting? On the other hand, since cows are calm beasts, we could always eat a little beef to even things out. But what about bravery? Where can we get lions to eat? Or tiger flesh? Especially since we've been eating all that chicken.

Who was it that said, "You are what you eat"? And what has he been eating?

TWO DIETS

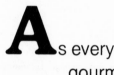

As every gourmand knows, the consumption of calories, or the enjoyment of food, bears a direct and somewhat ugly relationship to the state of one's figure. This is oftimes called the obese-ratio. Prolonged overeating leads to pronounced overweighing, which leads to the inevitable undereating, or, ultimately, being on a diet.

Finding an effective and pleasant diet is not easy. Notice that within the word diet is another little word—die. Notice also that *et* is a noun suffix occurring in diminutives. For example: A pocket is a small pock, a Chevrolet is a small Chevrol and a cadet is a small cad. What that means is the *et* makes the definition of diet clearer. Death means to die. Hence to diet means to die a small death.

Neither of us is a stranger to the rigors and sorrows of dieting and, during our cumulative lifetimes, we have lost a cumulative 978 pounds—and promptly found them again. No one can call *us* careless.

When it comes to diets, we have tried them all. We have even been on the ill-fated Matching Grant Diet for two semesters. For every pound we lost, the Ford Foundation gave us another.

We have contemplated, but not attempted, the acupuncture

diet based on the principle that it's difficult to eat with a needle stuck in your tongue, and we have for some time now been trying to patent a product that we think will work very well. It's called Diet Draino, "Melts the Pounds Away!"

One of the reasons it is so hard for us to diet is that we are crazed dessert people. We live for dessert. You could say we eat for dessert. You could even say that we would kill for dessert.

This is why we were thrilled to read about the latest in fad diets. It's the *7-Day-Candy-and-Anything-Sweet Diet.* This diet was invented by Dr. Smiley Dextrose, a man who brushes his teeth with sugar while singing "What Kind of Fool Am I?" It's been endorsed by the Sugar Society, commonly called the SS, and the Fresh Bakers Institute, commonly known as the FBI. It has also been hospital-tested, hospital-approved.

THE 7-DAY-CANDY-AND-ANYTHING-SWEET DIET

Breakfast
Two melted Hershey bars on a bed of lettuce.
(Syrup optional)

Lunch
A frozen Heath bar under whipped cream.
One daiquiri.

Dinner
Two pounds of sweet pickles.
One glass of kumquat juice.

Late-Night Snack
A half a pound of candy corn.

The reason you lose weight on this diet is this: As your teeth deteriorate, it becomes too painful to eat. Voila! A svelte figure and a disgusting smile.

Diets like this one are what make life worth living for us land

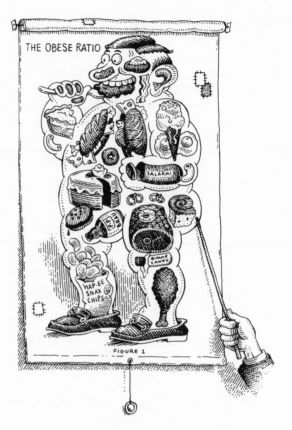

THE OBESE RATIO

SALAMI

POP BRAU

GIMME CANDY

HAP-EE SNAX CHIPS

FIGURE 1

blimps, but there are others less fortunate who never get to experience the ineffable pain of reducing. They are called thin people, and they feel left out. Everyone else is suffering acute diet pain but them. It is not fair, and that is why we are going to be the first to publish the *High-Calorie/Low-Satisfaction Diet*. This diet is designed especially for people who would like to experience all the hunger, emptiness and agony of being on a diet *without* the attendant loss of poundage. This diet absolutely guarantees to keep your weight up and your spirits down. It strongly appeals to people who subscribe to the Protestant Ethic (which comes out twice a month) and who prefer pain to pleasure and suffering to well-being. Here it is:

THE HIGH-CALORIE/LOW-SATISFACTION DIET

Breakfast

Peanuts (roasted, ¼ pound)	660 calories
Cup of Cocoa (made with whole milk)	245 "
Total so far	905 "

Lunch

Hungarian Pâté	
(2 lbs. lard lightly rolled in paprika)	230 "
Pine nuts (¼ pound, shelled)	676 "
Total so far	1,811 "

Dinner

Link Sausage (4 oz., cooked)	538 "
Pistachio nuts (¼ pound, shelled)	676 "
Grand total	3,025 "

You may have noticed that this diet is nuts, but so is anyone who tries it.

If you look in the **Larousse Gastronomique** you will find the following information under the heading **Punch:**

1. English seamen invented the drink in the mid-sixteenth century.

2. On October 25, 1599, the Commander-in-Chief of the entire English navy, a man named Sir Edward Kennel [sic], gave a punch party for his ships' companies.

3. The punch was made in a huge marble basin and consisted of 80 casks of brandy, 9 of water, 25,000 large limes, 80 pints of lemon juice, 1300 pounds of Lisbon sugar, 5 pounds of nutmeg, 300 biscuits, and something called a great cask of Malaga.

4. A ship's boy floated on this sea of punch in a rosewood boat and served the drinks.

5. The boy had to be replaced several times because each one was intoxicated by the fumes after fifteen minutes.

6. There were 6000 guests.

THE CIA
IN PEAS
AND CARROTS

We'd been hearing
about the CIA

for some time. Not the Central Intelligence Agency in Washington—everyone's heard of that—but the more secret CIA, the Culinary Institute of America, a school for chefs in Hyde Park, New York, seventy-five miles north of where we live, which features a restaurant known as The Escoffier Room.

We'd also been hearing about the HCC. Not the Harmony Carpet Corporation of Third Avenue—everyone's heard of that —but the Hartsdale Canine Cemetery, a place where mankind's furry loved ones are interred, located in Hartsdale, New York, twenty-five miles north of where we live.

And since it was summertime and the livin' was easy, we decided to hop into the old '53 Lincoln convertible, drive north and kill two birds with one stone. That is, visit the HCC and the CIA in a single excursion—feed the spirit and the stomach with the same tank of gas.

At first glance these two institutions appear to have nothing in common, but if you examine things a little closer, you will see that this is not true. They are both monuments to love, the highest forms of love that people know: the love they have for good food and the love they have for the dumb beasts who accompany them through this vale of tears we call life. And both places are deeply committed to the animal world. At Hartsdale the animal is buried. At the Culinary Institute it is cooked and eaten. At both places the animal is dead (except for oysters on the half shell, which are always eaten live).

"Let us go to Hartsdale, you and I,/ Where animals are buried after they die. In the tombs the women come and go/ Speaking of Bowser, Rover and Old Fido," we sang as the car sped rapidly along. In a short while we were at the Hartsdale Canine Cemetery, which is really the "Hartsdale Canine Cemetery, Inc. For all pets, birds. An historic Animal Burial Ground in Westchester, Est. 1896. Beauty and quiet. Visitors welcomed."

The Hartsdale Cemetery is a beautiful place. In fact, as we approached it, it struck us as one of the best-tended, prettiest cemeteries we'd ever seen. Here is a parklike place, rising upon a large, terraced hill. On the terraces are flowers and lawn, bushes and trees, graveled paths, and here and there, almost everywhere, stone monuments over the graves of the eternal slumberers.

As we passed through the iron gates and looked about us, we could find nothing to distinguish this place of animal rest from the loveliest places of human rest, until, after going on for several yards, we found before us a very large granite stone with the word G R U M P Y on it in bold roman, ten inches tall. We stopped to appreciate that, and then we proceeded on.

The next stone to catch our attention and our hearts was one that read

DOG
October 28, 1916–July 15, 1925
SHE LIVED TO LOVE

We walked on and discovered

BOOZIE COURTLAND
A cat so very dear

We passed

KING
An aristocrat

And

BUBBY
Mommy's Little Shadow
For 17 Years

And

MUGGINS 1936–1949
and
JILL 1948–1963

Even though our hearts are broken,
This to you is our last token

Our hankies left our pockets and found our noses. Two walking tubs of grief, we stumbled up a hill.

At this point grief had given us an appetite, it always does, but we decided to continue for a little while longer.

It was then that we found a treasure, something for our memory scrapbooks, a remarkable tombstone that conjures up a different age, a more genteel era, violins at teatime, feather boas, silk stockings with clocks in them, Murads, Melachrinos and Mazda light bulbs.

Beneath this stone is buried the
Beautiful Lion Gold Fleck,
Whose death was sincerely mourned
By his mistress Princess
Lwoff Parlaghy
New York 1912

We figure the Princess for a blue-blooded Russian madcap who drank vodka from crystal goblets and smashed them on marble floors with her tiny feet, and who must have been the center of conversation among the other guests in her hotel when she rode the elevator with Gold Fleck on his leash. Poor Gold Fleck, to live and die so far from the sunlit, grassy veldt of Central Africa, or, in this case, the sunny, windswept steppes of Mother Russia.

62

We passed on, so to speak, and paid dutiful respects at the site of one superlative, flamboyant gesture. The tombstone read

> Here rest their Master's ashes,
> With his two inseparable pals,
>
> 1924　TIMMIE　1931
> 1924　TEDDIE　1940

We wondered how his relatives must have felt going to his funeral and seeing him buried amongst the dogs and cats and monkeys and horses and parakeets.

And on that note we bade farewell to "Big Blitz, Nephew of Strongheart," and all the other friends of man who are interred here as a tribute to the love they gave and the love they received. They are missed.

Having done the cemetery, we turned our noses north and headed up the Hudson Valley to the CIA. We passed up several opportunities to eat along the way and took our journey fasting because to come to the Culinary Institute with a full belly would be vulgar if not gross, and God knows we are neither. What we had on our minds was a fast tour of the Institute and a slow meal at the famed Escoffier Room, manned entirely by senior students.

The Culinary Institute is the only private, nonprofit vocational college in the United States whose curriculum is devoted exclusively to culinary training. There are 1350 full-time students who, after successfully completing the four-semester, two-year course of study, receive an A.O.S. degree, Associate Degree in Occupational Studies (or, Always Order Stuffing), and who embark upon careers in the food-service/hospitality industry, which embraces hotels, restaurants, inns, cruise ships and hospitals—anywhere, in fact, where people are paying good money to take their ease and eat.

After driving for about an hour or so, we reached our destination, turned left off U.S. 9 and entered the grounds of the CIA.

The Culinary Institute is a beautiful place. In fact, as we drove up the approach road, it struck us as one of the best-tended, prettiest Culinary Institutes we'd ever seen. And indeed it looks like a place of higher learning—rolling lawns, shady trees, and a large no-nonsense academic building designed in the Hudson Valley/Jane Eyre School of Architecture.

We parked and started across the parking lot only to be brought up short—nostrils akimbo—struck by a gust of aroma. Aroma was everywhere: aroma in the parking lot, where it flowed amongst the silent, hulking cars; aroma amongst the bushes and trees; aroma that rolled down to the banks of the Hudson; aroma on Route 9, where it floated to the edges of Poughkeepsie. It was the smell of bread baking, of meat roasting, of spice spicing. It was the Culinary Institute at full simmer. Our feet did their stuff as aroma's long fingers of temptation reached deep into our noseholes and drew us along into the building and up the stairs.

Joan Doyle of the Institute's public-relations staff, a jolly, chunky, Dickensian woman who loves life and all the good things that go with it, mainly good food, had agreed to give us the cook's tour. We met in her office.

"Our kids learn how to make it and how to dish it out, in other words, the impeccables of good serving," she told us, taking a hit off a whipped-cream dispenser and giggling. "Now, do you want to stand here and chew the fat, or would you like to see the plant?"

We opted for the tour.

The first thing we noticed about the Culinary Institute when we drove up had been the aroma that surrounded it. Now as we followed Ms. Doyle down the corridors, the second thing we noticed was the size, shape and demeanor of the average *chef-aspirant*. None of the students resembled leading men. Most of them looked like character actors, character actors who were doing a strange play. In the first place many of them are overweight. At the Culinary Institute a little fat on the meat is desirable. In the second place they wear bandages that cover a variety of cuts and burns acquired under fire. In the third place they are all dressed in white. In the fourth place many of them wear hair nets by order of the State of New York. (The plot of this play escapes us, but we'll think of it one day.) And in the fifth place, these girls and boys look happy. Yes, that's right, girls. More and more, young women are going into cookery, and at this writing sixteen percent of the students were female. The way the world is shifting these days, a woman's place *can* be in the kitchen.

We asked Ms. Doyle what kinds of problems the school faces instructing these kids.

"Lack of experience. They don't know enough food. No familiarity with different cuisines. Some of the kids come here and the most exotic thing they've ever eaten is pizza."

"Pizza can be very exotic," we volunteered. "In Los Angeles, Pizza Man ('He Delivers') makes a pizza with a whole-wheat crust."

"No wonder they have earthquakes out there," said Ms. Doyle.

By this time we had reached the kitchen theater. Here the students sit in seats which rise up around the arena in ascending tiers and observe the master chef go through all the steps of a basic recipe. A mirror suspended over the work counter affords the students an optimum view of the chef's busy hands and the way he deals with the materials.

"What is he making?" we whispered.

"Looks like a ragout," answered Ms. Doyle.

The chef professor chopped an onion quickly, skillfully. "Now you see it," said Ms. Doyle as the onion collapsed under the cuts of the knife. "And now you don't."

When the ragout was ready the students came down, took little white paper cups in hand and waited in line for a sample of the finished product.

"That's so they'll know what the ragout is supposed to taste like," Ms. Doyle told us. "Tomorrow they go into the kitchens and make it for themselves. This way they'll be able to tell if they've made ragout or if they've made garbage. One of the things the CIA does is educate the student's palate. If he or she can't taste how can he or she cook? And now let's go and talk to the chef."

"What do you call this course, anyway?" we asked brilliantly.

"Well, this would be an entrée," the chef answered, somewhat confused.

"No," Ms. Doyle corrected him. "This course of instruction. What is it called?"

"This is Culinary Theory O1," he answered. "It's the first basic course. In the beginning there's a lot of note-taking, a lot of theory. A lot of going over, repeating, repeating, repeating. They say there's too much repetition, but you can only learn the basics by repetition."

"It's like playing the scales on the piano," Ms. Doyle explained. "You just have to keep doing it. Then, later, you can do the variations."

"Cooking is an art. It really is," the chef went on. "If you lined up twenty of our instructors and gave each of them the same recipe to follow and locked them each in a separate kitchen, you'd wind up with twenty different items. Because one likes salt a little more, somebody else likes a certain spice. It's very individual, it really is. Kids sometimes get confused because, you know, I show them one way here, and then they go into another course and the chef says, 'What the hell does he know'? and he tells them his way, and they wind up with ten different ways of doing it. Which is excellent, because you can't go out into the field on a job and say this is the way the CIA did it. The chef'll tell you to go to hell."

"We only teach basics here," Ms. Doyle said. "After that you start writing your own cookbook. Every student leaves with his own cookbook."

"Another thing we teach them is that you have to try everything," the chef told us. "*And,* very important, you have to taste everything you make. You can't really in all honesty send anything out that you haven't tasted yourself."

"What if a student doesn't have good taste? I mean, what if he prefers bad-tasting food?" we asked. "Does he go to work for a restaurant that serves rotten food to customers who have rotten taste and prefer rotten-tasting food?"

"A student who is determined to make bad-tasting food will not last long enough here to be graduated," said Ms. Doyle. "It is just not possible. There are usually a variety of good-tasting ways to make a dish and that is acceptable, but bad-tasting, well . . . in a way, it isn't easy ot make something bad-tasting if you use first-rate ingredients."

"Not easy, but possible," we said.

"Possible, possible," everyone agreed.

On this quavery note, we thanked the chef-instructor and headed for the door. As we reached it, we heard a student say, "Please, sir, can I have some more?" And as we passed through the door, we heard the crack of the ladle against the boy's ear as the chef-professor gave him a whack for his impudence.

Yes, we noted, there was definitely something Dickensian about this place—in the jovial sense of the word, of course.

Out in the hall again, we noticed way, way down at the end a small, dapper man in his seventies advancing toward us.

"Ah, it's Mr. Salomon," exclaimed Ms. Doyle. "Jean Henri Salomon, Chef-Instructor, one of the most illustrious faculty members." She ticked off his credentials: "Educated in Europe; Chef Garde-Manger, Carlyle Hotel; Yale Club: Executive Chef, Sherry Netherland and Gotham Hotels, New York City; Westchester Hotel, Washington D.C.; Princeton Club, New York City; Commanderie des Cordons Bleu de France; Certified Executive Chef of the American Culinary Federation. A lifetime in food service."

We were impressed.

M. Salomon had now reached us. *En passant,* he informed us in his charming French accent, "I am looking for my student."

"Tell these nice people something," said Ms. Doyle.

M. Salomon stopped, pondered for a moment and said, "You can tell most people in America put food in their stomach the same way they put gas in their tank—only they are more selective about the gas." Then he was off looking for his student again. We wished him the best.

The next place Ms. Doyle took us was the school storeroom where the supplies are kept, and where we learned that the CIA normally keeps a quarter of a million dollars' worth of food on hand. The place really looks like a small supermarket. We wandered up and down the aisles, enjoying the boxes, cans, packages, bottles and noodles as the student in charge recited the litany of weights and numbers.

"The school uses up one hundred forty-two point five gallons of milk a week, thirteen thousand, three hundred twenty eggs a week, four hundred thirty-two pounds of chicken a week," he intoned.

Chicken reminded us of a prediction made by Winston Churchill back in 1930 in an article he wrote for *Popular Mechanics.* We thought it was funny and decided to share it. "Sir Winston Churchill," we said, "predicted once that by nineteen-fifty, 'we shall escape the absurdity of growing a whole chicken in order to eat the breast and the wing, by growing these separately under a suitable medium.' " We laughed. No one else did.

"Can you imagine the sight of thousands of plucked breasts hopping to the trough to feed?" we said. "Or little pathetic wings working themselves like scissors, flipping and flopping to get to the food?" We laughed again. The others smiled politely.

"We go through about ninety-six heads of iceberg lettuce a day," the student continued.

We realized that we'd laid an egg with Sir Winston's chicken story. No one likes to know the great are foolish.

The student went on. "We consume thirty pounds of garlic a week. And five hundred and six pounds of butter. We also use a lot of truffles." He took us into his office and showed us the safe where the truffles are kept. And it's true. From the array of canned truffles that we saw, it was obvious that they must use a lot of truffles—all from France. Either that, or they just keep a lot of empty truffle cans on hand.

He also showed us a can of something called trufflettes. "A trufflette is an artificial truffle," he explained. "Actually, if I remember right, it's eggs, charcoal and something else. It's black, it's the shape of the can and it's just like a black cylinder, which you slice very thin and it looks like a real truffle."

"What does it taste like?" we asked.

"Charcoal," he replied imperturbably.

"Oh dear," we said. "Is this stuff palmed off on people instead of real truffles? Are people paying real-truffle prices and getting a no-truffle product?"

"Oh no," he said in horror. "It's used only for decoration. It's put *on* things, not *in* them. You don't eat it—it tastes like charcoal." The student sat down, eyes aghast, and tried to catch his breath.

"Come with me," said Ms. Doyle. "I'll show you the trufflette in action. Next stop, Buffet Catering!"

One of the skills learned in buffet catering is how to make a log cabin out of butter. We were fascinated. Anyone woud be. (The problem with a butter cabin is that it might be difficult to keep up at the height of summer on the lake, and would it keep you warm enough in deepest winter? At any rate, it would keep you greasy any time.)

Buffet catering is devoted to the art of the hors d'oeuvre, the aspic, the galantine, the pâté, the terrine, the preparation of forcemeats and sausages. And also to ice sculpture, but more of that later.

This is the area of highly decorated food, the domain of the radish tulip, the redoubt of the egg daisy, the home of the salmon rose, the herring and shrimp orchid, your very own name spelled out in chopped liver, or, if you will, more complex representations such as Lindbergh Landing in Paris or the Raising of the Flag at Iwo Jima. We recalled a tribute to General MacArthur on a large, flat meat loaf where the egg salad on MacArthur's hat was real egg salad, the fruit salad on his chest was genuine fruit salad, his corn cob pipe was made entirely of tiny, pickled corns on the cob, and his slogan, "I shall return," was written in finely braided pimento.

It is in these tableaux that the trufflette sees its highest glory. The trufflette is cut into shapes and carefully placed to represent the black parts of these pictures. Think of how much trufflette would have to be used to make a Groucho Marx face, or even worse, the Smith Brothers, Trade and Mark? Using perfectly good, tasty, *expensive* truffles in this way would be a real waste. Escoffier might have used truffles for this purpose, but he cooked for kings.

The day of our visit the students in Buffet Catering 1 (two credits), twelve boys and one plucky girl, were preparing for their initiation into the ephemeral art of ice sculpting.

The chef-instructor told us that very few of them ever get to be good at it. "But it's part of their education. A lot of these kids are hoping to move into supervisory positions in the restaurant or catering fields, and they'll need to know how much to demand from others and how much to expect."

The students showed us their sketches. Several of them were planning to make swans, always a popular favorite. One boy was planning to render a duck, and someone else was planning to make Frosty the Snowman. We were planning to watch.

But since their preparations were going to take a while, we left the Buffet Catering kids to their cooling off, and followed Ms. Doyle to the faculty lunchroom, where the Intro to Food Service kids were warming up and getting ready to handle napkin, silverware, plate, tray, glass, pitcher, decanter and carafe as they served faculty and guests (us) the lunch that other students had prepared with their own scorched fingers only moments earlier: roulade of beef and other tasty things.

Ms. Doyle took us to a nice-looking, middle-aged man who was giving instructions to a harried student. The student, now even more harried, rushed off immediately to perform some task or other, and Ms. Doyle said to us, "I want you to meet our Mr. Bully. He really isn't a bully, he's a pussycat."

Mr. Bully said, "I am not a pussycat; I am a bully," and smiled.

We said, "How do you do," and sat down with him at one of the tables.

He told us that in his previous life—his life before coming to the CIA—he had been *maitre d'hôtel* for some of New York's largest restaurants.

He told us that waiters in large and very busy restaurants communicate across the vast spaces by means of hand signals, which are preferable to shouting, an activity beneath the dignity of a man in a tuxedo. One of these signals, we unfortunately can't remember how it goes, means, "Put this stiff on ice and send him to Siberia; the bum never tips." Others indicate things like "Table for four free," "The customer who just came in is the owner's cousin," and "Where is the damned busboy?" Mr. Bully, we were learning, was full of wonderful information.

He also told us about a well-known and high-priced restaurant in New York that has rats. They do not serve rats, but they have them. In fact, at closing time, after the lights are turned off, the main dining room becomes a no-man's-land that none of the waiters dares traverse. They call it vermin territory.

Mr. Bully's conversation was making us very happy. So happy, in fact, that we forgot to notice what we were eating, or how much—plenty. And the moral there is: Good conversation is the enemy of food.

The rest of the afternoon flashed by in an exhausting round of visits to exotic classrooms. We saw students "learn by doing" in ten production kitchens, four workshops, two garde-manger laboratories, two auditorium kitchens, ten classrooms, three instructional dining rooms, two wine-and-spirit classrooms, a butcher shop, a commercial storeroom, the largest library of cookbooks in the country, a real roadside student-operated diner/coffee shop, and an *haute cuisine* restaurant. The future chefs study everything from cost control to advance meat cutting and menu French.

A visit to the pastry division was a special treat for us. There were wonderful samples to sample, and while we were there we spoke with Chef-Instructor Albert Kumin about one of his specialities and one of our favorite examples of human effort that is both awesome and foolish: cosmetic baking, baking for display and competitions. This is elaborate, decorative, architectral, fantastic, creative bakery, fired like a brick, intended to endure. As in Buffet Catering, we were once again in the province of the *tableau non-vivant,* and, in this case, non-edible. What we are talking about are *pièces montées* such as replicas of the Empire State Building, three feet high in sugar; spun sugar swans or dancing peasants; or even a complete miniature bathroom created entirely out of meringue. (We swear this is true—this marvel was wrought for a plumbing company's annual banquet.)

But the biggest thrill of the afternoon was coming upon the

good old Buffet Catering kids out in the sun, chopping away at their blocks of ice as quickly as they could because the ice was melting as quickly as it could.

The ice event had become a party in the parking lot. Everybody was hard at work, hacking and chipping and giggling and hooting. The sun was warm, the ice was cold, everybody's feet were good and wet, and there were little puddles of water all over the place.

All of the ice works looked the same, with variations. The swan looked like Frosty the Snowman with a lizard growing out of his head, the duck looked like Frosty the Snowman with a tail and Frosty the Snowman was getting smaller by the minute—it was Frosty the Incredible Shrinking Snowman.

The day was growing to a close. We were all tired, and Ms. Doyle's voice was giving out. There was nothing for us all to do then but wait for dinnertime in a corner of the bar, which is named The Rabelais Room, sip some wine and exchange lusty, bawdy and ribald tales with some of the staff members.

We grew maudlin, sentimental and philosophical, and told the group about our earlier visit to the Hartsdale Canine Cemetery. Then we observed that the CIA was almost a metaphor for life. It is devoted to incredible effort which produces things that do not last. The food gets eaten. The ice sculpture melts. The sugar edifices crumble. Ashes to ashes, dust to dust. Sweets to the sweet. Gone and regrettably forgotten. There should be memorials to such pleasures and delights.

Someone suggested a monument to a Beef Wellington he had eaten once:

> THERE IS AN OLD BELIEF
> THAT ON SOME DISTANT SHORE
> BEYOND THE SPHERE OF GRIEF
> OLD FRIENDS SHALL MEET ONCE MORE

Then Mr. Efron suggested a large statue of a jumbo shrimp with the inscription

> GONE, BUT NOT FORGOTTEN

And Ms. Olsen added a tribute to a miraculous dish of green

semolina gnocci she'd eaten at the Gritti Palace in Venice:

IT IS ALWAYS NEAR MY HEART

All too soon it was time for dinner.

The Escoffier Room is an elegant, formal dining room, open to the public, which serves a prix fixe dinner for $14.50—wines are extra. We are happy to report the dinner was excellent, we enjoyed it enormously—good food, well cooked, the freshest ingredients (the kitchen boasts a live trout tank and what could be fresher than living fish?).

A special charm and piquancy was added to the affair by the student waiters and waitresses. One boy had a lot of trouble serving a steak fillet with some kind of topping—perhaps a ball of parsley butter. The topping kept sliding off the steak onto the plate; he kept putting it back on and it kept sliding off. Meanwhile, on the other side of the room, two waiters bearing water collided and spilled some on themselves. Later, we watched a girl cut a piece of layer cake, put it on the plate upright and have the top layer fall over.

Whether these novices will be the Carêmes, the Escoffiers and the Colonel Sanderses of the future, only time will tell. But it is clear right now that they are trying hard to learn to do it right, and, one thing *we* had learned during our visit: a lot of love and enthusiasm on the part of the faculty and the student body was going into the process. So why shouldn't they be great? Failing that, they sure were having fun and there are worse ways to spend your life than in food. Going without food, for one.

TAKE
THIS TEST,
PLEASE

Television
advertising
often features product-testing stunts. In the course of testing
the product some unusual recipes are recommended. We decided to try some, but after several days of nonstop TV view-
ing, we saw so many tests of all kinds that we felt we had to deal
with more than just the recipes.

The thing about these tests that is different from the kind you
knew and loved when you were in school is that these tests
are not supposed to be taken. No one in his right mind is expected to take them. No one in his right mind would want to
take them. No one in his right mind invented them.

These tests are designed to convince the potential consumer
of the advantages of the product being tested and, often, of its
superiority over Brand X, or, in these days of the new morality
(traveling down the hang-out road), the explicitly named competing brand. Also, no manufacturer is going to show his product losing or coming out second best, which leads us to believe
that these people will go to any lengths to win.

Another thing about these tests is that they are either so complex, or so time-consuming, or so difficult, or so foolish that the
manufacturer and the advertising-agency people can all sleep

nights safe in the knowledge that no one is going to test their test and call them on it—except us.

We did it. We tested the tests. For the sake of science we went to the supermarket and purchased a strange list of groceries, sometimes two of the same item, sometimes different brands, with every intention of wasting all of it.

We began with the Wesson oil test, which is subtitled: Man does not live by bread alone, there's got to be a little oil in there somewhere—but just a little. The point of this test is to show that Wesson oil fries only the outside of a loaf of bread and none of the oil penetrates past the crispy part.

In this commercial a skeptical teenage girl takes a loaf of unsliced white bread, trims the crust and fries the soft part in a pot of hot Wesson oil. When the bread is fully fried, she removes it from the oil and cuts into the loaf. The interior is not greasy. It is white and pure as the driven snow. The teenage girl is no longer skeptical. The test has proven that Wesson oil does not penetrate food. We set about to duplicate this situation and see for ourselves.

The first challenge: Find a loaf of commercial bread that is not pre-sliced. With some difficulty—and a great deal of ready money—we met that challenge. We were able to locate sixteen ounces of Pepperidge Farm's finest whole wheat, unsliced at twice the price. Forging ahead we filled a large pot with over two dollars' worth of virgin Wesson—that's Wesson that's never been kissed by the flame. Next, with cold-hearted, surgical precision, we sliced the crusts off the loaf. We were left with a denuded, pathetic, vulnerable-looking crustless brick of bread. Over on the stove the oil was heated, and it was time for the moment of truth—the big plunge. Taking the unforgettable tongs (tongs for the memory) in hand, we picked up the specimen and thrust it into the hot Wesson.

In a very short time the bread acquired a crispy brown crust. It looked delicious, and when we pulled it out, it smelled delicious. We drained it on an entire roll of Bounty, which we had because we planned to take the Bounty test later on. The excess Wesson penetrated through to the tenth layer of the Bounty. We considered this ominous. The next step was to cut into the bread and see how deeply the oil had penetrated it.

76

It grieves us to announce that the test was a failure. The grease, gasp! was present to a depth of one half inch all the way around. Not what we'd seen on television! Yet, as the old song tells us, every cloud has its silver lining, or conversely, every silver lining has its cloud. The bread smelled good. The bread looked good. And when we applied jam and jelly and marmalade and ourselves to the bread, it tasted good. The Wesson people have a damned good recipe here. It could be popular except that it is expensive. And so, this is what America has come to, a country where only the rich can eat fried bread for dinner. Nonetheless we think that deep-fried Pepperidge Farm unsliced whole wheat is the greatest thing since sliced bread.

For our next test we turned to the kitchen sink, which we had cleverly lined with tea bags and blueberry jam to produce what they call "those hard-to-get-out stains." We were going to test Comet's stain-removing powers against those of Ajax!

Unfortunately before we could apply the cleansers, we turned on the hot water—with a disastrous effect. "Those hard-to-get-out stains" vanished under the hot water within seconds. The test was a washout. "To hell with this test," we said, and to perk up our spirits after this fiasco, we thought it might be nice to eat again.

We decided on a quick breakfast/lunch. Total vs. Quaker 100% Natural. These two cereal-type breakfast foods are matched against each other in another popular television test. The question posed: Do you really get one hundred percent of your mandatory requirements of vitamins and iron from only one ounce of Total compared to twenty-five ounces of Quaker 100% Natural? Answer: We don't know. We never found out. We're not scientists. But we did take *our* test. One of us ate one ounce of Total. The other ate twenty-five ounces of Quaker 100% Natural with lots of sugar in it. Both had milk.

Question: Which one was happier?

Question: Which one gained weight?

Question: Now which one is happier?

Answer: The one who ate the twenty-five ounces of Quaker 100% Natural with sugar, silly. Twenty-five ounces of anything

is going to make you happier than one ounce of something else. Especially if you're hungry.

The next test was difficult and challenging. We thought that the Efferdent Denture Cleanser test would be as easy as pie, as easy as blueberry pie. This is the test that bakes a set of pearls made of denture material inside a blueberry pie and then cleans the stains off with Efferdent. All we had to do was find a set of pearls made out of denture material and bake them in a blueberry pie. Nice and easy. We went all over the city looking for them: Tiffany's, Cartier's, Woolworth's, Van Cleef and Arpels'. Harry Winston said he could let us have something in sapphires. Nobody had any pearls made out of denture material.

Next step: We called our friends. None of them had any pearls made out of denture material. Then, early in the afternoon, the solution was found. One woman friend allowed as how, though she didn't have any pearls made out of denture material, she did have a set of her mother's pearlies, uppers and lowers. She said we could borrow the teeth on the condition we got them back to her in good shape because her mother was returning soon from the Bahamas and would be needing them. We agreed. Now we were really happy. We had our test material: a friend's mother's teeth. And we had our pie: Sara Lee blueberry.

You have no idea how hard it is to get a set of dentures into a ready-made, frozen blueberry pie. And you have no idea how much harder it is to eat the pie after you've gotten the set of dentures into it and baked them. But we did it.

As for the teeth, we removed them from the pie after they'd been baked and they looked awful. They looked like big losers in the Gleem suck-this-discoloring-tablet-after-you-brush-your-teeth test. Exactly what we'd been expecting.

We plopped the stained, hot, sticky false teeth into a measuring cup with an Efferdent tablet. It was like a blue Alka-Seltzer. And we're proud to say the teeth were cleansed, the water was cleansed, the glass was cleansed. We don't know what happened to the schmutz, but in any case, the crud was gone. Eaten, apparently, by the Efferdent. And then, the Efferdent disappeared. The water went as clear as it was before all this started. We still can't figure it out.

The next product we tested was Bounty, which is always used at Rosie's Diner, where the customers are always spilling things. We think, by the way, that Hollywood is going about it all wrong with big disaster movies. We think that what audiences would really like to see would be movies about disasters that ordinary people can relate to, more down-to-earth disasters like *Spilled Ink, Lost Keys, Torn Pants,* or *A Meal at Rosie's Diner.*

There are several basic tests at Rosie's Diner. One: Can you spill this? Two: Can you make a mess? Three: Is Bounty the quicker picker-upper? Four: Can a wet towel support two cups of coffee and two saucers? We tested all of the above. We are happy to announce that Bounty *is* the quicker picker-upper, which is to say, Bounty really sucks. We did the parfait-glass test in which a paper towel is expected to absorb all the coffee in a parfait glass. To prove that it does, the towel is stuffed into one such glass and the glass is turned upside down. This is is done with a Bounty towel and with another leading towel. With Bounty the coffee is absorbed, with the other towel a lot of the coffee runs down out of the inverted glass. When we did it, Bounty did absorb more liquid quicker than the other towel tested. The only thing about our test that was different from the one on television was the amount of coffee we spilled on our clothing when we inverted the glass with the failure-towel in it. We christened this the Brown Badge of Courage and went on with our investigation—which is why we can say with authority that a wet paper towel held between both hands will support two cups of coffee if one cup is piled on top of the other, but basically, a wooden tray is handier. We don't recommend paper-towel trays for formal tea parties either; they are ugly.

And now we come to our last test. It had nothing to do with food or with the kitchen, but we wanted to try it because it was difficult and complicated. It required initiative and ingenuity. This test was the Calgon Bath Oil Beads test. If you've seen this on television, you've seen a pair of identical twins taking baths in their bathroom, which contains two identical bathtubs. The twins are testing the greasiness of bath oil—Calgon vs. another leading oil. In the commercial the Calgon twin is incapable of leaving a greasy mark on a mirror when she is fresh from her bath. But the twin that used the other oil does leave a smear on the mirror when she touches it with her finger.

We couldn't find any identical twins who were game for the test. The closest we could come to identical twins was a pair of nearly identical cousins, Heidi and Ofra Torkelsen, and to find a gamier duo, you would have to go a long way.

That was one problem solved. We were still, however, faced with the bathtub dilemma. Where would we find two bathtubs in one place? We looked in the yellow pages and located Sam, the Plumberman. He had a lot of tubs and sinks and toilets and was only too happy to oblige as long as we spelled his name right. It is Sam. S-A-M.

Sam set the tubs up in his window, side by side, in tandem, identical twin tubs, if you please. We put Calgon in one and an unknown but leading oil in the other, and Heidi in one and Ofra in the other. We added water and we were in business. The employees and some of the customers gathered around to watch and formed a ring around the bathtub. The girls enjoyed their baths and everyone enjoyed watching them enjoy their baths. This was a fun test, but ultimately the girls got a little waterlogged and pruney and we had to bring the test to its conclusion.

"Time for evaluation," we said. "Get the mirror." Sam did not have a mirror. Without a mirror, we didn't know how we were going to find out which girl was greasier. At this point, some of the workers volunteered to touch the girls and sign affidavits attesting to the relative greasiness or lack of greasiness of their epidermi.

Well, it wasn't strictly by the book or by the TV, but we were in a pinch and something is always better than nothing. Ofra and Heidi agreed, and the fellas formed a line and one by one they touched Ofra and Heidi. The boys had a good time, but it didn't work out so well for us. The twins got so dirty, and greasy too, from all this handling that we had no way of knowing whether Calgon was greasier or whether the other leading oil was greasier. The girls got fed up and rushed home to take baths. *Sic transit* Ofra and Heidi, Calgon and the other leading oil. But it was a hell of a party while it lasted.

And so, to conclude. We were not able to take all the TV tests. We were unable to arrange for a diamond cutter to demonstrate his art in the back of a moving Mercury, we did not weigh competing paper towels (but we are ready to bet that Aunt Bluebelle is heavier than any of them), we couldn't quite bring ourselves to pour water on Pampers or Kimbies paper diapers and we refrained from unleashing competing toilet-paper rolls to see which was longer. However, we feel that one thing was proved, and one thing only: Fried bread is great; too bad we can't afford it.

What is kosher and not kosher? Were you wondering? Did you think you knew? Have you read your Bible lately? We quote Leviticus 11: 2–23 (American Bible Society Revised Version).

All winged creeping things that go upon all fours are an abomination unto you. Yet these may ye eat of all winged creeping things that go upon all fours, which have legs above their feet, wherewith to leap upon the earth; even these of them ye may eat: the locust after its kind and the bald locust after its kind, and the cricket after its kind. But all winged creeping things which have four feet, are an abomination unto you.

Let us tell you about those locusts. The Biblicals ate them with relish. And they ate them often and they ate lots of them. They boiled them, they dried them and they ground them up into powder, or preserved them in honey or vinegar. Locusts taste like shrimp, we've been told, and are a good source of protein, so ask for them at your neighborhood kosher butcher.

SOME
CAME RETCHING,
or
QUAT DESCENDERAT
ASCENDERATI
MUST

There is another side to the pleasures of eating. That is the problem of effluence, the flip side of food. Or, to be more explicit, getting rid of it once you've ingested it. Every once in the while when we've eaten too much and find ourselves suffering from the hard belly, we also find our minds turning to meditation on that all-time monument to the joys of gluttony, the Roman vomitorium.

Vomitoria, by the way, in case you never took Latin in high school, were the places where, during dinner, Romans went between courses to lose their cookies. Human capacity, even then, was limited, but not human ingenuity, greed or lust, and that's how the vomitorium was born. Eat the first course, tickle your palate with a feather, disinfest your stomach; and now you have room for a second course. Simple and brilliant.

The vomitorium, alas, has gone the way of the chariot races, and too bad. Now when the need strikes, what does an ordinary citizen do? What are his alternatives? The potted palm in the corner behind the sofa where he has been ditching his cigarette butts all evening? The toilet bowl? The kitty-litter box? How about the elevator shaft, or over the edge of the balcony? These are problems which the ancient Roman glutton did not have to face, and who can doubt that his legendary strength of

character, steadfastness in battle and self-confidence did not
arise, in part at least, from knowing that when he needed it it
would be there? It is worth the trouble to think about.

Once the subject of vomitoria arises and we allow our minds
to muse upon its whys and wherefores, certain questions bub-
ble up. Important questions. Questions like

1
Where was the vomitorium located?
How far from the dining room?
(If it was too far from the dining room,
the food would get cold while you made the trip.
If it was too close,
it would have a depressing effect
on everyone's appetite.)

2
How many could use the vomitorium
at one standing?

3
How was the room laid out?
Were there stalls for privacy,
or was it a group effort?

4
What about footwear and the problem of tracks?
Did one change one's sandals,
wear hip boots, or go barefoot?
And were the boots called up-chukka boots?

5
Was there art work on the walls?
And if so was it meant to be inspiring or uplifting?
Was it mosaic, fresco or ipecac?

6
How many times during a meal
does one visit the vomitorium?
And how many times can you do it in one meal
and still eat the dessert?

7

Were there attendants and did they accept tips?

8

Why has this civilized practice been allowed to die?

One day last May these questions got to be too much for us and sometime toward the middle of June we went to the public library in search of answers. By the end of August, we had found none of them and concluded that the vomitorium is one of the better kept secrets of the ancient world. We did, however, learn a great deal about Roman mess habits that is both astounding and illuminating and which may explain the need to have invented a vomitorium.

The ancient Romans gave to gluttony a new dimension, hitherto unknown in the known world. A dinner wouldn't be your mundane soup-salad-entrée-dessert-nuts-and-coffee affair. Your Roman dinner might be soup, salad, twenty-four main courses, dessert, nuts and coffee.

The citizens of Ancient Imperial Rome were crazed for quantity. What we call the "good and plenty" syndrome—if it's good, there should be plenty, or if there's plenty, it must be good. With the Romans ostentatiousness was a religion. God knows what Thorstein Veblen would have made of them. This was not merely conspicuous consumption, this was consumption that beat you over the head and gave you a headache you couldn't forget.

Romans had feasts in which the fishes and birds that were served numbered in the thousands; these dishes had nothing else to recommend them but their exorbitant cost. One of our favorites is a mixed grill, which used the tongues of five thousand birds that had first been trained to speak.

What can you say about a cuisine that includes such savories as dormice fattened on nuts, eels restricted to a diet of living slave meat, flamingo brains creamed into a fine paste, wild sows stuffed with live thrushes, red wine mixed with spices and sea water? You can say, "Please pass me the feather."

Seneca remarked that his countrymen ordered foodstuffs from all over the world and then did not even deign to digest them. Among those who did not deign was Vitellius, the Glutton Emperor.

Vitellius, who reigned for only one year, A.D. 69, loved to eat more than any other human who ever lived. He had an appetite that wouldn't stop. Vitellius ate oysters four times a day, twelve hundred of them at each meal. That's five thousand oysters per diem, and that would fully occupy anybody's stomach, to say nothing of the two thousand choice fish and seven thousand choice birds he is reported to have eaten on at least one state occasion. Vitellius clearly had a problem finding room for his Minimum Daily Requirements or, in Vitellius' case, his MDE—Minimum Daily Excess, and that's where the vomitorium came in handy. Lucky for Vitellius it was there.

If Vitellius represents the flesh of Roman Eating, Heliogabalus represents the spirit. He invented the first dinner theater. It must have been lovely. When one course was finished, the table would sink into the marble floor and young slave boys would sing to it. We like to imagine them as being somewhat like the Vienna Boys' Choir—their limpid, angelic voices producing crystalline notes of unspeakable beauty as their peach-down cheeks flutter in cadence. When the table had finished its downward course, Heliogabalus would have heavy Oriental perfumes wafted into the room to clear the air. And we like to imagine that this would add to the overheated atmosphere and inspire the diners' hasty departure for the vomitorium. For the remainder of the intermission, dancers would fill in the time with erotic dances, an appropriate choice on top of a heavy meal.

This was followed by the Radio City Music Hall part of the program. As the Vienna Boys' Choir raised their voices in sham surprise and squeals of amazement and sincere astonishment—"Oh gosh!" "Gee Wow!" "Ai Caramba!"—the table would reappear out of the floor like a mushroom loaded with goodies.

When that course was finished, the table would sink again, the slave boys would sing, there would be more perfumes and another hasty trip to the vomitorium. What showmanship! Heliogabalus, we salute you! Of course, without a good-sized vomitorium, this form of entertainment would be quite impossible, and we can be sure that Heliogabalus had a vomitorium much in keeping with the quality of his dinner.

Some of the Roman food itself seems to have promised certain gastric upheaval and may have occasioned an unprogrammed visit to the vomitorium. Take, for example, garum. Garum was truly ubiquitous. The men and women of Ancient Rome used it on everything. It was to them what soy sauce is to the Chinese and Miracle Whip is to us. Here is the recipe. (Judge for yourself and see if you don't think this would lead anyone to the vomitorium.)

Into a container (not aluminum) place the entrails of many fish—it does not matter what kind—salt them well, leave exposed to the air until fully decayed and putrid. Drain off all of the liquid, and save. Discard the rest. The liquid is the base for garum. To this base add any or all of the following condiments: dill, anise, hyssop, thyme, rue, cumin, poppy seeds, shallots, onions, garlic, or anything else you can think of.

Garum, which is also called liquamen, is supposed to have a cheesy flavor before the addition of the spices and condiments. One authority claims that when you've eaten garum, you don't sweat. You can't sweat, no matter how much you want to. We believe that it also causes you to talk without moving your lips, but we're not sure about that.

All of the ancient Roman meals did not offer sensory disturbance. Some were emotionally wracking. Take for example the Lucullus guilt-trip dinner. Lucullus was terribly refined, and one of his most delicately conceived dinners was a rare and subtly unsettling fish feast.

An exquisite glass jar containing a live trout or mullet was placed in front of each diner, who could then watch his dinner die before his very eyes. He whose fish leaped last was assured that his was the finest since it had been the friskiest. When all the fish were dead, they were taken away and cooked. Then they were brought back to the table and eaten. Later that night the diner could reflect upon the accusing look in his fish's eyes, the noble effort with which the fish attempted to continue living despite the fact that all life support had been removed; and the length and breadth of the fish's suffering. And, also, if one were a true Roman, one could do a little extra suffering because Marcus Agrippa's or Quintus Gallius's or Marullus Maximus's fish had lasted longer.

86

It does not take much to imagine a Roman diner alone hours after the feast in his *lectus* (bed) stewing over his fish, his fish's last gasps and the pain his fish must have suffered. Even while he digests that fish (and all the other morsels from the table), the fish gets his revenge and our Roman is on his feet and moving fast. And if you asked him, *"Quo Vadis?"* (Whither go-est thou?) he would have to answer, "The vomitorium and I can't talk now."

Then there was Trimalchio's feast, another kind of emotional wringer. This one employed the Trojan Pig, and was immortalized in Latin by Petronius, a cultured and literate man. Later, other cultured and literate people translated Petronius's work into English. All of these writers had a tendency to improve upon the original and give the dialogue a more elegant tone. However, the truth is that Trimalchio was the worst sort of arriviste, nouveau-riche, spendthrift sport. The following is a truer account of what happened about one thousand, eight hundred and seventy or so years ago.

Imagine, if you please, a large Roman dinner party. The guests are reclining on their couches, parsley wreaths around their heads. They've already eaten seventeen courses—and are they hungry! "What's next?" shouts Asiaticus, one of the invited guests. "We're wasting away. I'm ready to put on the feed bag."

"Here, here," seconds Priapus. "I can hardly wait."

With that, Trimalchio claps his hands three times, hits a gong and pulls a bell rope.

Afar off, distant chimes are heard. There are the sounds of footsteps coming closer. The guests begin to clamor more loudly and are just getting out of control, when . . . the curtains part and what to their wondering eyes should appear but four slaves bearing a huge, heavy platter containing a mammoth roast pig.

Gnaeus is the first to speak. "Oh boy," he says. "Let's eat."

"I've got dibs on the knuckles—all of them," says the over-eager Priapus.

"Pig snout for me," cries Gaius Flavius, the well-known epicure.

Trimalchio calms them, saying, "Don't worry. There's enough to go around." Then he stops short, stares in wide-eyed horror at the roast pig and cries out, "By Jupiter, what's this? Hasn't this pig been cleaned out?" He examines the roast more closely. "May the gods give me constipation, it has not!" he exclaims. He calls for the cook. "Where is that miscreant, that low-life, that perpetrator, that I may salt his hide!"

The cook, Spiculus, trembling and wretched, is brought in wringing his hands and his tunic and sweating profusely. His knees knock against one another till they turn to jelly and he sidles to the floor.

"Stand up," says Trimalchio, "and take your beating like a professional. Take off your tunic and prepare yourself for the kiss of the kurbash," he continues. "Fifty lashes and then a pound of salt."

The cook weeps and pleads for himself. The guests join in,

"Yes, spare him, spare him. Let's get on with it, we're hungry!"

Trimalchio grows dignified. "My guests have spoken," he says. "Who am I to contradict the laws of hospitality? Spiculus, you are spared but not forgiven. You must clean this pig now in front of our guests," he tells the cook.

"Yes sir, yes sir," says the grateful cook, kissing Trimalchio's knees before putting his tunic back on.

Now a new servant suddenly appears and produces a purple velvet pillow with a carving knife on it. The guests try to conceal their disgust. The cook seizes the knife gleefully and plunges it into the pig's belly. The skin parts wide open immediately from the pressure behind it, and out plop multitudes of sausage, black puddings, squab, thrushes, steaks, chops, roasts and what have you. For, yes, you guessed it, this is the Trojan Pig!

Doctors tell us that quarreling at the family table—discussing religion, politics or money—agitates the digestive juices and leads to discomfort, dyspepsia, heartburn and assorted other minor but disquieting ills associated with poor digestion. What then must have been the state of Trimalchio's guests' digestive tracts after one of these hectic, rough-and-tumble meals? Probably not very good. Even though styles in clothing and food may change, the human machine remains the same. We can only conclude that Drusus, Germanicus and the others made ample use of the vomitorium.

And now, lest you think that Roman table manners were all vulgarity, we'd like to tell you about the *mappa*. Some Roman contrivances were big and some were small. Some are gone from us forever and some are very much with us today. Take for example the Roman *mappa*, the forerunner of the modern napkin.

The *mappa* was a piece of cloth that guests brought with them to the dinner, banquet, feast, orgy or wedding party. It started out simply enough in plain white toga muslin, 60 stitches to the inch, but as Roman decadence bloomed and flowered, blue became the favorite color and 180 stitches to the inch the rule rather than the exception. Gold fringe was also favored by the chic.

The *mappa* was used to wipe the fingers, the lips or the chins —these people were big into finger foods and you know what that can mean. Eventually there was another use for the *mappa*. Occasionally a diner found he couldn't eat everything that was put before him, no matter how many trips he'd made to the vomitorium, and, with his host's permission, he would put the uneaten portion into his *mappa* and have his slave carry it home. Thus the Romans inadvertently invented the doggie bag. Let's give credit where credit is due.

Mouse milk costs $10,000 a quart.

This is the worst thing we've ever heard of:

SARDINE RAREBIT

1 box sardines	toasted bread
onion juice	2 egg yolks
lemon juice	6 teaspoons melted butter
salt	⅛ teaspoon beef extract
2 tablespoons grated cheese	paprika
1 tablespoon thick cream	lemon quarters

Remove bones and skins and pound sardines to a paste. Add a few drops of onion juice and lemon juice, a dash of salt, the grated cheese and cream. Toast bread, remove crusts and cut into narrow strips. Spread the sardine mixture on one side of strip and place another strip of toast on top. Set in oven until sauce is made. Beat the yolks of two eggs. Add to them the melted butter and beef extract. Beat until the mixture begins to thicken. Add salt and a dash of paprika. Turn the mixture on the strips which have been kept hot in the oven. Serve it at once with quarters of lemon.

HOW WE
LEARNED TO OVERCOME
SIBERIA PAIN
AND MASTERED THE ART
OF DINING OUT

ating in fashionable

restaurants is a frightening experience for most people. It used to be hell for us, especially since we always ended up sitting in Siberia. Siberia is the place restaurants seat customers who might embarrass them or customers whom they wish to punish for not being good enough. It is a lot more than just a cold shoulder and glacial stares. It is physical isolation and emotional desolation. It is also often near the kitchen, and that is too degrading for words. God knows what horrors you might discover when you can see into that interior. The mere possibility puts such a chill over the heart that no matter what you eat it doesn't taste right. But the true, worst thing about Siberia is that being put there brings your basic inferiority to the attention of the other, more acceptable diners. For years we suffered from Siberia Phobia and avoided fancy restaurants until we realized that our year in food was drawing to a close and that we had yet to experience Haute Cuisine Française in Haute Cuisine Française surroundings.

Not knowing which restaurant was what and what restaurant was which, we called our friends in the retail garment industry for their recommendations. They eat out a lot on expense accounts.

We were told, "Don't go near La Côte Basque, the last seven times I ate there I was disappointed." We were also told, "You'll love the Palace, it'll run you a C-note apiece, the dining room is small, but don't pay any attention, the ceilings are high." However, it was not until we talked to Barnett Zetzel (he used to be Sam Zetzel, but he changed his name legally to Barnett in 1966) and were told, "Go to Le La Lela, it's definitely classical French, with the most imaginative cook in New York and not too expensive," that we picked up the phone and made a reservation.

Then we confided our fears to Barnett and told him that this was going to be one restaurant experience that wasn't going to get us down. We were going to act like big-time people—we were going to be arrogant. We would never smile, we would look down our noses, and, just so they'd know whom they were dealing with, we would wear all our labels on the outside of our clothing: Halston, YSL, Bill Blass, Dry Clean Only and the Wool symbol —a lamb chop with hair on it. Those snobs at Le La Lela were never for one moment going to think that we were not born with restaurant cutlery in our mouths.

"No, no," said Barnett, "that's all wrong. You're thinking about vulgar places for the nouveau riche. Real class is always nice. The people at Le La Lela are obsessed with fine food, its preparation and its presentation. Wear nice clothes so they'll know you're not clods, but don't overdo it. Smile a lot and say thank you. Pretend you are the Queen of all the Englands and the French Dauphin. Remember, the more simple-minded and giddy you are the more likely you will be taken for royalty, and treated accordingly. Never forget that it is the restaurant's job to serve and delight you and that your job is to reward them with elegant smiles of gratitude, a multitude of thank yous and a handsome tip."

We were dubious and would have debated the subject more but, since M. Louis of Le La Lela had told us that he could squeeze us in if we came promptly at six o'clock and since it was already five-fifteen, we promised that we would give his approach a fair trial and bustled outside into the bumper-to-bumper rush-hour congestion and grabbed the first cab that stopped for us. The cab driver, who considered giving signals a sign of weakness and changing lanes laterally a sign of movement, got us there fifteen minutes late. We were nervous, frazzled, sweaty and terrified that M. Louis might turn into an Indian giver and take back the reservation and we would be shamed in front of a room full of sophisticated eaters. We stood at the door for a mute second and our courage began to fade. Frown lines criss-crossed our brows. We remembered Barnett's advice, "Pretend you are the Queen of all the Englands and the French Dauphin," so without courage but with a foolhardy kind of zeal we prepared to take the plunge.

Once indoors our eyes glazed over from fear, but, nevertheless, we smiled. We smiled at the brass umbrella stand, we smiled at the wallpaper, we smiled at the framed awards hanging on the wallpapered wall, and we smiled at M. Louis, the maitre d' of Le La Lela, who smiled back at us and gently and solicitously led us to the hatcheck woman, who turned out to be Madame Lulu of Le la Lela. Madame Lulu returned our smiles, tenderly helped us peel off our slightly damp coats and turned us over to M. Louis's custody again. M. Louis led us, the two late-comers, into the dining room, which was totally empty. We looked at M. Louis. He explained, "If we did not start with you this early, we could not accommodate you at all. After you have been here a while you will understand." He smiled. We smiled. He seated us dead center. Dead center, although a very unsettling location in an empty restaurant, could never be Siberia.

M. Lyle, our waiter took us over. We smiled at him and asked him what was good to eat. "Oh, la, la," he said. "What it is to you that the choice is left." We smiled some more and tried to look as agreeable as possible. We smiled at the flowers and feigned delight. The busboy, Lionel, noticed and ran off to return with some more flowers which he placed on the table in a heap. This was turning into a somewhat different experience. We smiled at the thought.

When we opened the menu, we immediately noticed the restaurant's motto. On the left side of the menu was written in French, "Art is Patience." On the right hand side of the menu was written, "Cuisine is Art." Quickly putting the two thoughts together we realized that the solution to the equation goes like this: Art is Art, therefore if Patience equals Art and Cuisine equals Art, Patience equals Cuisine or Cuisine equals Patience. Therefore, this was going to take a long time.

The bread and the wine, nevertheless, were promptly served, and we nibbled and sipped as we waited for the appetizers we'd ordered. The knowledgeable M. Zetzel had instructed us that the truffle in pastry was something special and well worth the additional ten dollars above the twenty-dollar prix fixe the dinner was going to cost us. We ordered one of those and also the genuine foie gras (the fat liver of the force-fed goose) in sauce Véronique that would also cost an additional fee. For entrées we had ordered Beef Wellington (a French favorite named after a major defeat and not before) and Medallions of Veal (named after nothing in particular).

We were just polishing off our first bottle of wine and watching the seven o'clock diners straggle in when suddenly we heard a skirmish at the kitchen door—bumpings and whisperings and what sounded like a small physical struggle or a minor fight. The door flew open and two men appeared. They were kitchen men, for they were dressed in white and wore small white muffin hats. They seemed to be holding back a third man, our waiter, Lyle, who was wheeling a small cart. Then it seemed they failed, for he broke loose and rapidly wheeled his cart across the room toward our table. He too was dressed in white. The three men, now very excited, made their way to our table and displayed for our approval what was on the cart.

What was on the cart came as a total surprise to us and everyone else in the room. It was a sailing ship, like a galleon, made entirely of toast. All the pieces of toast were evenly tanned by the oven to exactly the same color and had been cunningly cut and attached to each other to make up the decks, the bulkheads, the Captain's bridge, the galleys, the stem, the stern, and the poop. Little sticks representing the masts pierced pieces of toast representing sails ballooning in the wind.

We looked at it, the ship of toast, and looked at the three men who had brought it, smiling of course. That is, we were smiling and so were they. Our thoughts raced wildly. Was this the truffle in pastry? And if so, wasn't this toast and not pastry, and how would we eat it? We would need a pound of butter to get all this toast down, and then how would we eat the rest of the meal?

"What do you call this?" we asked.

One of the men answered proudly, "The S.S. *Truffles.*" Then two of the men bowed and, smiling, swept back to the kitchen with the S.S. *Truffles.* The last man, Lyle, remained holding a tray that had been previously concealed in the bottom of the cart. On the tray was the truffle in pastry. The S.S. *Truffles* had steamed our way just to deliver it.

We dug in and it was superb. Yes! This time we actually tasted and experienced the earthy, musty, gorgeous, expensive ecstasy nugget. There is nothing like it. It is very special, very sophisticated, and when it somes surrounded by *duxelles* (a mushroom hash) in a flaky, croissant-like pastry, it is divine.

However, the foie gras was better. It was so delicious that our eyes closed involuntarily and our throats produced little rapture-squeaks. We had never tasted anything so rich or so smooth. All the cholesterol money can buy and worth every penny. To eat it is to be divinely blessed in a state of joy rampant upon a field of napery. Only good manners prevented us from taking our plates and going back to the kitchen to beg for more.

After the foie gras came the anticlimax: the rest of the meal, which was merely perfect. Why is it that the things you get to eat before you get to eat the things you eat are better than the things you eat? Someone should look into this.

This is not to say that the meal itself was negligible. It was remarkable. Perfect, white, tender veal sautéed in butter, covered with a delicious sauce and with various vegetables cooked to perfection. And the Beef Wellington was faultless. A tender, juicy, lovely filet of beef surrounded by pâté and covered with a flaky pastry outside.

During the meal the cook came out of the kitchen and walked around the room, stopping at every table to inquire after the food. There were no complaints. His name, by the way, was Leo. Chef Leo.

We polished the meal off with raspberry *sorbet,* coffee, and kisses. Real ones, not chocolate. Our exit was a veritable love feast. We hugged M. Louis. Madame Lulu hugged us.

95

It matters not where we are seated,
Just so long as we are fêted.

La Salle de Yakutsk

Lionel and Lyle ran over to exchange kisses. Chef Leo joined them. It was tearful. It was spectacular. Farewell Le La Lela. Farewell Louis, Lulu, Lionel, Lyle and Chef Leo. Oh God, what a meal. What a restaurant. What service. What lovely people. Too bad we can't go back. If only we'd remembered to leave the tip. Fortunately New York is full of good restaurants, and we were over Siberia Pain and Siberia Phobia forever.

The next week we went to another posh place and were immediately seated in Siberia. Deepest, darkest Siberia. There were empty tables between us and the nearest customers. It mattered not at all. We behaved with perfect noblesse oblige and took the staff by surprise. We were the Grand Duke and the Dowager Empress. We smiled, we were very silly-headed, we were extremely gracious, and they responded in kind. The service we received was impeccable. In fact other diners picked up their plates and glasses and moved closer to us so they could bask in our light and maybe get a little service too. Of course, we left no tip. It would be unfair to Le La Lela.

DINER ENGLISH

Adam and Eve on a raft: Poached eggs on toast
Two, with their eyes open: Two eggs sunny-side up
Two, on a piece of squeal: Two eggs with bacon
Twelve, alive on a shell: A dozen oysters
Bossy in the bowl: Beef stew
Tube steak: A hot dog
Stars and Stripes: Beans and franks
Boiled leaves: Tea
Red noise: Tomato soup
One splash: One cup
Dough well done, cow to cover: Bread and butter
Eve with the lid on: Apple pie
Rabbit food: Mixed salad
Oinkers: Pork sausage

When it comes to camel meat, connoisseurs prefer the hump, the feet and the stomach. The hump we can understand. It is all fat. It is not a water sack like you've always thought. As the camel treks across the desert wastes, his system breaks down the fat cells in his hump to get at their water content and uses it. A high hump means a happy camel. A floppy hump indicates a thirsty camel—and a thirsty camel is an unhappy camel. About the camel's feet and stomach, we know nothing. They are a mystery to us.

Connoisseurs consume the hump of very young camel after it has been marinated with oil, lemon juice, salt and pepper and roasted exactly as if it were sirloin of beef. The hump of old camel is discarded and not cooked at all. Nor is it eaten except by very hungry people. Connoisseurs are never hungry people.

Camels' feet are served in an oil-and-vinegar dressing. The dish is known officially as **Pied le Chameau à la Vinaigrette.**

The best stomach dish is called **Ventre de Chameau à la Marocaine** and all we know is that it is cooked for a long, long time, because cooking it is better than eating it. In fact, this is how Moroccans keep thin; they look at the camel stomach in the pot and say, "Let it cook some more." After a while they look at it again and say, "Let it cook some more." And so forth. They hardly ever actually eat it.

Moses, by the way, forbade the Children of Israel to eat camel, but Aristophanes maintained that camel was served to royalty. However, he wrote comedies and is not to be trusted.

97

Appendix

For those who wish to pursue the subject further
or have special problems
that need help and/or assistance.

COME EAT WITH US!

THE ESSEN INSTITUTE
For taste awareness
sensitivity training
and
appetite-appeasement therapy

THE ESSEN INSTITUTE presents weeklong, weekend, one-day and
evening workshops in a dramatic natural setting at Lake Dunphy
in the majestic Adirondacks on eighty acres of sanitary,
hygienic cooking facilities.

* * *

"What is LIFE for, if not for Essen Geh Essen?"
—Dr. Henry Penny, Ph.D.,
Director, Friend,
Chief Cook and Bottle Washer

* * *

WHAT DOES ESSEN GEH ESSEN MEAN?

Essen geh essen is an Algonquin name for something indefin-
able in the English language. The purest definition lies
in that instant when the impact of the flavor of a given
morsel of food registers in the sensory center of consciousness,
but no later than that moment when the involuntary mechanism
governing the muscles associated with the process of swallowing occurs. And since our own cognition of our personal
awareness of the consciousness of taste is important to us, so
is that function and process all over the world, the universe,
and perhaps even the larger population centers of the West
Coast, important to all sentient beings everywhere.

THE PURPOSE OF THE ESSEN INSTITUTE

The purpose of ESSEN is that each person accept, without
guilt, the responsibility of his or her own taste.

THE CREDO OF THE ESSEN INSTITUTE

We at ESSEN believe that taste is a lifelong process,
that we will all taste for as long as we live, and that it is
our right as human organisms to strive for better emotional,
intellectual, physical, spiritual and artificial flavor.

* * *

101

There's a special thrill, a special knowledge to be gained
from gobbling up wisdom at the feet of the masters, developers
of new therapies. And that is why we have added six courses
to our curriculum this summer. We know you won't want to
miss these exhilarating experiences, so we are sending you
this reminder now to register right away.

All workshops have limited space, so sign up early.

The Open-Gestalt-Sandwich Workshop
Dr. Benjamin Hippenhammer, MSG.

A weekend marathon filled with discovery. The focus is on
what is IN your mouth now, rather than what was, might be,
should be, could be, would be, need be.

"Do I have permission to eat, or must I wait with my hands
folded, my napkin in my lap? Do I eat what I want when I want
it? Eat what I think? Eat what I show? Eat what I tell?
Or do I eat what others expect of me to eat? Are my parents,
teachers, waiters, maitre d's, busboys, hot-dog vendors, still
inhibiting/inhabiting me? Do I eat at the depth of my being,
or am I eating a "should be?"—Dr. Hippenhammer's description
of food-anxiety neurosis. Sound familiar?

By using psychosimmering techniques and various cuts of
choice meats and selected fruits and vegetables, explore with
"Ben" Hippenhammer what you eat, and who, and more important
how to prepare it/them.

Passive-Palate Therapy   Otto and Lena Titzling

A week-long journey toward more sensitive eating.

This workshop will focus on seasoning as a therapeutic agent
in appetite growth, as a way of discharge of conscious and
unconscious flavors and as a means of zeroing in on one's
personal taste-bud hang-ups. No experience in tasting is
required; however, participants are invited to submit samples
of various spices and herbs which have given them pleasure.

(Please do not send perishables ahead of time in unmarked
packages, as we do not store food. Last year several people
who took the Bio-Taste Therapy Workshop sent perishable goods
in packages a month or two prior to registration and there
were some heavy odors.)

We will begin with a historical review of seasoning as a
taste amplifier from pre-barbeque society to the present—
from its early shamanistic tradition, through its use both in
Etruscan cuisine and during the golden age of Greek souvlaki,
and to its continuing use in drive-ins today.

We will then look at the theoretical basis of seasoning as a
tenderizing modality (Adolph's), as a vehicle for self-
expression (garlic, nutmeg), and interpersonal exploration
(mushrooms, artichoke hearts, jalapeño peppers), along with
consideration of the countertherapeutic possibilities (Tabasco
sauce over coffee ice cream.)

The week will end with stress on chewing while eating, with
emphasis on the process of digestion. What could be more
natural?

Food Interpretation for Beginners   Anne O. Dine
    Learn to interpret your own leftover food. Use this power
to find out about yourself, and amaze your friends, solve
problems, find lost keys, experience other dimensions. Read
the future from chicken entrails and tea leaves, then eat
them. Later, you will work with leftover spaghetti, water-
cress salad, and develop proficiency with coffee grounds and
egg shells. The future is here now. All you have to do is
learn to read it.
    (This year we take pleasure in welcoming a new faculty
member, "Annie O," to Essen. "Annie O" spends most of her time
in the future—as anyone would have to admit after speaking
to her. For the past four years she has been living in
Europe, studying various approaches to eating, tasting,
working with groups, plants, and animals and loving a man.
Now that they have called it off, she is back. "Annie O" was
one of the founders of The Center of Tomorrow in Belgium and
Finca La Fonca in Spain. She does reading and personal
advising in New York at Grass and Roots, a popular salad
restaurant, and studies with Orwell Abend at his Institute for
the New Creature Man.)

Shiva and Shakti: A Jungian and ESSEN GEH ESSEN
Approach to Self-Digestion   Doyle Lishness, A.I.D.
    Shiva is the masculine, receptive dish: beef, potatoes,
apple juice. Shakti is the feminine, active principle: salad,
salmon aspic, cottage cheese. These two menu forces are
almost without parallel in Western Thought, which generally
understands the concept as: masculine/aggressive/high carbo-
hydrate and feminine/passive/light dishes, no gravy. And this
is the starting point of our workshop. We will explore the
most masculine of eating habits—cake or pie with milk—and
the most feminine—a single slice of fried liver with a cup
of tea.
    Essen and Jungian approaches are blended through tantric
weaving of the opposing forces in an Osterizer—cake or pie,
milk, liver, tea. Participants will be obliged to eat this
mixture, thereby activating the reactive forces which flow
through all of us, and be guided thereby into a fantasy male/
fantasy female personality dynamic.
    A better integration of self-taste will be the outcome of
the course.

"Lonely Chowhound" Peer Support-Group Structures
Dr. Alton Starr, M.A.
    Here is a seminar-and-workshop-orientation program people
have been asking for for the last three years. This seminar/
workshop fills the gap left when Power Trips at the Table was
discontinued because of certain people's behavior patterns.
Dr. Starr conducts an easygoing program as a medium for self-
directed personal-growth matrices involving eating in public
places without causing a disturbance.

"Lonely Chowhound" therapy focuses on why
1. Some of us are left to eat alone and don't know why
2. Some of us fear dining in public
3. Some of us cannot eat unless we have a newspaper
4. Some of us are afraid of food
   All of these problems and more will be explored in a light-hearted atmosphere of sharing, comfort, mutual respect and appetite appeasement.
   At the end of the seminar the group will move to the great dining hall for workshop exercises.
   First you will eat a meal facing a stranger who will interact with you through a series of novel, relatively nonthreatening "games," such as "Who has the fork?" "Where is the salt?" "Pass the sugar."
   Once the procedures are mastered, Dr. Starr will introduce an exciting set of structured experiences involving fantasy and touch designed to expand and sharpen your taste-control mechanism in the presence of others and permit you to chew with your mouth closed. There will be peanut butter.

Dinner Psychodrama   Dr. Henry Penny, Ph.D.
   A weekend experience for the entire family.
   Participants work out their fears, dreams, longings and special recipes before a paying dinner audience.
   Activities include cooking, taking orders, serving, busing tables, remembering who ordered what, set-ups, keeping water glasses filled, maintaining a cheerful disposition, not smoking behind the counter. Longhairs must wear hair nets and all tips will be pooled.

* * *

We are also offering seminars in tangential areas, such as designing a texture pattern for a light dinner for six: Avocado salad, chili (with or without beans), chocolate pudding, tomato juice and communicating with other species on this planet.
   There will be sign-up lists available for further activities. Groups will be formed for: Hatha Yogurt, Wolfing, TMM (Transcendental Menu Meditation), Primal Eating (mainly custards) and Primal-Taste Confrontation Therapy designed to release the Primal Burp.

* * *

We love people here; many of us came here for the first time and stayed to watch others grow as we have. And having grown, some of us leave; others come to take our places. But as members of a shared community we leave with the knowledge that we have unfolded our bodies, minds and digestive tracts to something more than ordinary.
   Come eat with us! And then come back for seconds.

LET ME SHOW YOU
HOW TO CUT
YOUR EATING TIME
IN HALF AND
TRIPLE YOUR CONSUMPTION
IN JUST 5 DAYS!

‼ MASTER SPEED-EATING !
‼ BE A SPEED-EATER !

IT SOUNDS INCREDIBLE
but Evelyn K. Food Graduates can
eat a seven-course meal in four minutes!

At that speed 4,187 calories go down with more impact than a peach
pie covered in whipped cream.

WITH TOTAL RECALL OF EVERY BITE, OF EVERY MORSEL

You can do it too. So far over 55,000 other people have done it! People with different mouths, different teeth, different tastes. But they share one thing: appetite. The desire for food is sometimes called hunger. Our graduates are people from all walks of life, from every cuisine, with all kinds of taste preferences. These people have all taken the course and have tripled their eating speed—or even better—without changing their taste preferences.

Think for a moment what that means. All of them—even the slowest, pickiest eaters—now eat an average meal in under a minute! What a time-saver! And they remember every bite, every chew, every sip. They eat an entire candy bar or box of popcorn in less than a second. "I ate a Baby Ruth in less time than it took to take the paper off," writes Gene Marko of Rudley Rocks, Pa. "Then I ate the paper."

HERE ARE SOME OF THE SKILLS TAUGHT AT
THE EVELYN K. FOOD EATING DYNAMICS INSTITUTE

1. How to eat without chewing and swallowing
2. How to eat several foods at once
3. How to eat various foods in any sequence—ice cream, pickles, sardines, cream puffs, chili, steak, Cheez Whiz

4. How to finish everything
5. How to spit out bones or seeds while simultaneously taking in food
6. How to remember what you have eaten
7. How to eat up and down as well as from right to left across the plate

8. How to flex your jaws like a snake
9. How to eat strong and peppery, spicy foods fast without gagging
10. How to eat fat fast
11. How to pay the bill
12. How to keep track of what you've eaten
13. What to do for constipation
14. What to do for diarrhea
15. How to walk after a meal

Dr. Food will teach you her "steam shovel" technique. Also, tips on how to ingest food under pressure in a constant stream—and it works even for <u>Denture Wearers</u>!

<u>EVELYN K. FOOD GRADUATES ARE AMAZING</u>!!

Graduates of the Evelyn K. Food Eating Dynamics Course have been known to clear a Smorgasbord table in a period of well under two minutes. A team of three Evelyn K. Food Eating Dynamics graduate students ate out four restaurants and one diner in a half hour.

The chefs, the waiters, other customers were amazed as the graduates settled in for some heavy eating. When they were through, there was nothing left to eat! Yet graduate Melvin Kaminsky remembered every bite of every morsel and could evaluate in detail what he ate that he liked and what he ate that did not please him. <u>AMAZING!</u>

FROM OUR FILES

<u>Ted</u> <u>Holmes</u> <u>of</u> <u>Old</u> <u>Loaf,</u> <u>W.Va.,</u> <u>writes:</u>
"I was a picky eater before I attended Dr. Food's Eating Dynamics Institute. Now I eat everything in sight and all of it completely. Do I have an appetite? You bet. When I say I can eat a horse I am not exaggerating. I can and have eaten a whole horse."

<u>David</u> <u>Finkle</u> <u>of</u> <u>New</u> <u>Hump,</u> <u>N.H.,</u> <u>writes:</u>
"Thank you, Dr. Food, for your wonderful course. Two weeks ago I had the meal of my life: the hind quarters of a wildebeest garnished in potatoes and turnips—in all, a meal of 239 pounds. If it hadn't been for your Institute, I would never have finished and lived to eat the tail."

<u>Wyatt</u> <u>Earp</u> <u>of</u> <u>Tombstone,</u> <u>Arizona,</u> <u>writes:</u>
"Dr. Food and her Eating Dynamics Institute Course has given me more pleasure than words can describe. Just the other day I ate a nine-course meal in just under six minutes. When I gave my order to the waiter I told him

to bring everything at once. With the time I saved on
that meal, I went across the street and had a huge Chinese
dinner while all the time my brothers and friends were
only halfway through the second course of their first
meal. By the time they were onto their entrée, I was
finishing off a Mexican combination platter of 1 taco,
1 tamale, 1 enchilada, plus rice and beans. Evelyn K.
Food, thank you for an evening neither I nor my friends
will ever forget."

---

aster such eating techniques as The Hollow Leg, The Bottomless Pit
nd the Steam Shovel. Increase your intake capacity fourfold!

n additional course is available for postgraduates which shows
ou how to take advantage of neglected body pockets. Yes, store
aten, but as yet undigested, food in little-known cavities
istributed in various parts of your body. Evelyn K. Food
nstruction will show you special breathing procedures which allow
ou to retain undigested food for weeks and draw on it when you
ant it. Think of the time you'll save, and you'll have both hands
ree.

* * * * * * * * 100% MONEY-BACK GUARANTEE * * * * * * * * * *

    WE WILL REFUND THE ENTIRE TUITION OF ANY STUDENT WHO DOES
    NOT GET ENOUGH TO EAT OR WHO DOES NOT TRIPLE (300%) HIS
    OR HER EATING SPEED AS MEASURED BY A SIDE OF BEEF OR HALF
    A HOG. YOU EARN THIS GUARANTEE BY COMING TO ALL THE
    CLASSES AND BY PRACTICING EATING ONE HOUR STRAIGHT EACH
    NIGHT BETWEEN CLASSES THROUGHOUT THE SEVEN-WEEK PROGRAM.
    MY EATING-DYNAMICS COURSE WILL CHANGE YOUR EATING HABITS
    OR I'LL EAT MY WORDS.

* *

                COME TO FREE MINI-MEAL

                            EVELYN K. FOOD
                            EATING DYNAMICS INSTITUTE
                            BRIOCHE BUILDING
                            21-45 ALIMENTARY CANAL DRIVE
                            NEW PORK CITY, NEW JERSEY

A CLIP 'N SAVE INFLATION TIP

HAVE YOU NOTICED
YOUR FOOD DOLLAR IS BUYING LESS AND LESS?

Penny Crocker Says:

"MONEY IS CHEAPER THAN FOOD SO
PUT YOUR MONEY WHERE YOUR
MOUTH IS AND EAT IT!!"

Here's a batch of new ideas for good eatin'
that's quick 'n easy 'n fun:

SALAD

Render unto Caesar Salad—A lettuce-and-cabbage green salad.

Take several dollar bills (the crisper the better), tear into bite-size portions. Add root-of-all-evil, thinly sliced, a pinch of change and hint of the mint. Sprinkle liberally with palm oil. Toss lightly (sometimes called throwing your money around). Top with Bring-Home-the-Bacon Bits.

APPETIZER

Loan-Shark Num Nums That Gather Interest—If you have money to burn try these hors d'oeuvres.

Cut a fin in half and wrap it around a few clams. Bank for 25 minutes at 400°, or until edges turn brown. Garnishee with your salary.

MAIN COURSE

The Buckburger—Lip smackin' smackers for the whole family. The buck you cannot pass.

Grind up a quarter pound of food dollars per person. Add 1 nest egg and ½ cup of bread crumbs (shredded saw-bucks make the best crumbs). Moisten with bullion. Broil. Serve on poppin' dough. Ummmmm, ummm good! And legal tender!

DESSERT

Frozen Assets—Rich in flavor. A grand way to close out any meal.

Deposit a roll of C-notes in your freezer overnight. Withdraw just before serving. Sprinkle with cashews for an added dividend. Eat with a silver spoon.

If you run out of money, use your checkbook as a substitute. Poor people can eat their food stamps.

Eatin' money is nothin' new. The Poet in an oft-quoted and fav'rite poem written more than a hundred years ago tells us:

> "The Owl and the Pussy Cat went to sea
>   in a beautiful pea-green boat.
> They took some honey, and plenty of money,
>   wrapped up in a five-pound note."

So long (green) for now,

Penny Crocker

of *General Mils*

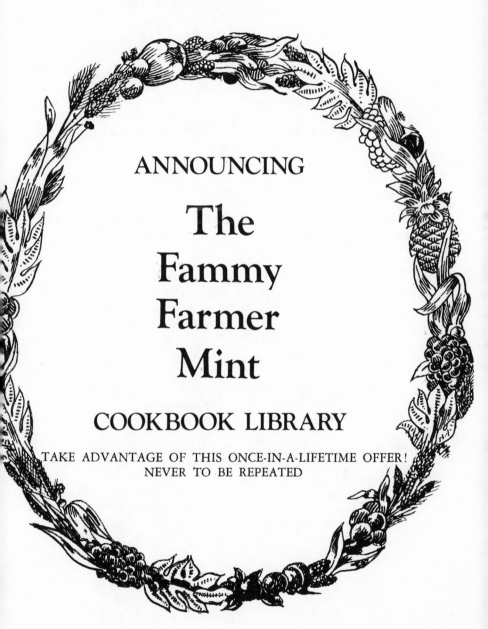

A COMPLETE LIBRARY
OF THIS CENTURY'S GREATEST
POT-BOILERS
CHOSEN BY A DISTINGUISHED
INTERNATIONAL BOARD OF SAVANTS

The Greatest Cookbooks of the Twentieth Century is a collection as earth-shaking and breathtaking as any in the history of rapturous publishing.

Ours is a century that has seen the works of more great cookbook writers than all the previous centuries combined. And yet only now have the greatest of these works of genius been brought together in a single, ultimate, definitive, luxury collection containing over 7,775,000 inspired, visionary masterpiece recipes.

The task of selecting these heroic epics of the griddle, oven and broiler has been entrusted to a distinguished advisory board of connoisseurs, savants and boffins. What is more the challenge of heading this unparalleled body of discerning *cognoscenti* has been accepted by John Hershey, the award-winning author of *A Bar for Adano* and *Hersheyma, with and without Almonds.*

EACH BOOK BOUND IN
GENUINE BEEF JERKY
(ORNAMENTED IN 22-KARAT GOLD)
CAN BE BOILED DOWN AND EATEN
IN TIMES OF TROUBLE

Each book will be designed to stand on its own. (No need for it to rest on a table or shelf.) Yet each book will look like all the other books exactly so that you and your friends will know they are from the same set. Some will be bigger than others and some will be a different color.

Each volume, moreover, will be fully bound in genuine beef jerky and intricately ornamented in 22-karat gold—making it a work of beauty that will attract the eye as well as the appetite. Lustrous moiré endleaves, carefully designed typography, specially milled bookpapers and full gold edging will add to the quality and enduring value of each volume.

Taken together, *The Greatest Cookbooks of the Twentieth Century* will constitute a luxurious personal library of lasting importance—a library that even the most ardent collector of fine volumes would find impossible to acquire in any other way.

THE FOLLOWING BOOKS ARE BUT A SAMPLE OF
THE RANGE OF THIS COLLECTION:

THE LADIES OF
THE DEPARTMENT OF HIGHWAYS
OF THE STATE OF MAINE
COOKBOOK

Compiled by Flora Shibles
and Alice Dunfee
Typed by Amelia Mullins
and Priscilla Needles
Proofread by Cora Clark
and Lorna Dorney
Overall organization
and planning
by Wilma Hitchcock, Sally Bonney,
Ruby Robinson and Mildred McKensie.

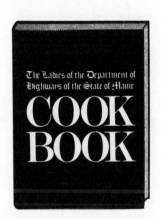

Important recipes of Maine's legendary cultural tradition: Nut Goodies with Whoopie Filling, Mashed Potato Donuts and Seafood Melody in Cream of Mushroom Soup.

HOW TO COOK TRAFE

Duane Higgins compiles for the first time in over 2000 years the classic ancient recipes for unclean food. Learn the secrets of the cheeseburger (combines dairy with meat) and in addition ferret stew, cooked chameleon, stuffed lizard California and uncloven hoof in aspic. Each dish is an abomination. 5000 recipes.

LES TECHNICALITIES
by Jack Pepper

This is not a recipe book. It is instead an unrivaled illustrated guide to the fundamental skills of cooking. Allows any cook to become as proficient as a master chef. Some of the technicalities explained include: How to slice salami on the bias, How to say "Have a Happy Day" in spinach or cole slaw, How to staple pimento smiles on mackerels when making mackerel-head stew (you don't want them frowning at you from the stew pot).

More than 7 photographs.

THE HERMITAGE HERITAGE
COOKBOOK

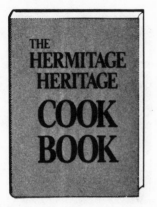

At last, the first and only definitive collection of great recipes of the men who lived alone and liked it on America's frontier, composed by Ned "Attaboy" Winks.

One chapter tells the story of hermits who meet once a year at the top of Mt. Wilson, carrying large bags containing all their old clothes. They gather at a huge cauldron of boiling water and throw in the clothes, which are steeped for twenty minutes. The hot water converts to juice all the spilled and dripped food that permeates these garments. The juice is skimmed off the top, allowed to cool and ultimately drunk by the assembled, restoring health and preserving life. The hermits go down the mountain and carry on till next year. Fascinating!

THIS IMPORTANT COUPON COULD CHANGE YOUR LIFE!

Dear Fammy Farmer Mint,

Please accept my subscription for *The Greatest Cookbooks of the Twentieth Century* consisting of one hundred volumes to be privately prepared, bound in genuine beef jerky and issued to me at a rate of one volume per day at the issue price of $38 for each jerky-bound volume—a mere $3,800 for the entire set.

I will be billed individually for each jerky-bound volume, in advance of shipment. I will pay the bill as soon as I receive it. I will not go back on my word. I swear all loyalty to Fammy Farmer. At Christmas I will send more money. Enclosed is an inventory of my net worth. Please feel free to take anything you want.

NAME _____

ADDRESS _____